D1559228

The
BUSINESS END
of Government

The
BUSINESS END
of
Government

by
Dan Smoot

WESTERN ISLANDS

PUBLISHERS

BOSTON   LOS ANGELES

Published by
WESTERN ISLANDS
Belmont, Massachusetts 02178

Manufactured in the United States of America

Contents

Introduction

Mao Tse-tung, the father of the Communist dictatorship in China, is widely quoted as having said: "Power comes out of the barrel of a gun." According to a recent report of the Senate Internal Security Subcommittee, Mao has used that power to murder nearly 64 million of his own people – many for no other reason than that owning a small piece of land made them capitalists.

Identifying the same principle, George Washington, the father of our country, observed: "Government is not reason; it is not eloquence; it is force." But Washington, loving liberty, devoted himself to binding down that force with the once powerful chains of the Constitution, defending the right of free men to live, produce, and prosper in a free economy.

It is therefore a curious fact that both George Washington and Mao Tse-tung would instantly recognize from its title what this book is all about. Simply put, the theme is that liberty is destroyed when freedom of enterprise is under the gun of government. President Washington loved liberty, and by warning of the business end of government assured freedom for millions.

Mao Tse-tung hated liberty, and applied the principle to destroy freedom and to murder millions. My friend Dan Smoot, the author of this book, is concerned that by their assaults upon the Constitution of the United States our leaders have turned from the course of George Washington to that of Mao Tse-tung. I believe Mr. Smoot is right, and that those of us who love America must do all we can to reverse this trend while there is still time to do so.

The book you are about to read by that distinguished commentator is the best general outline I know of how a regulation in an area remote from our own experience or interest can quickly spread to nearly all of our activities.

It has been published as part of a continuing educational effort of The John Birch Society, on whose Council I am proud to serve, but distribution of this book will by no means be confined to members of the Society. I know that thousands of businessmen who read it, some of whom will know nothing at all about the patriotic efforts of our Society, will also wish to purchase copies for their friends and customers. It should be read by all Americans who are interested in the protection of their freedom, and distributed among their friends. A suitable reference book is *The Invisible Government*, by the same author, and I do urge you to read both, and to get involved. For those of you who want to help with this important project quantity prices are listed on page 225.

American business, the most productive in the

world, and all of its customers (consumers) and employees are under the gun. And that gun is in the hand of a bureaucratic giant that is beginning to make Big Brother look like a pygmy. Recently the editors of *Industry Week* asked the federal Office of Management and Budget how many federal regulatory agencies are now operating, only to find there are so many that no one in Washington even knows their number. A year ago the *Federal Register*, in which the bureaucracy publishes each new executive decree, bulged to nearly as many pages as there are in the entire *Encyclopaedia Britannica.*

Congressman James A. Haley reports that there are now, at all levels, some 13 million civilian federal employees, snoopers, and bureaucrats of assorted stripes and scents, whose salaries alone cost us about $107 billion a year.

And this is just the tip of the iceberg. There are in addition a vast host of federal advisors. The Office of Management and Budget lists 1,724 consulting advisory commissions, including 40 added by the Nixon Administration. Congressional researchers contend that there are as many as 1,800 additional "outside" advisory commissions, plus another 1,400 "inter-agency" committees, advising the bureaucracy.

In order to satisfy the demands of these masters of regulation-by-decree, American business is being choked in paper work. Preparation of the forms they require is costing American industry as much as $75 billion a year, to which must be added the $10 billion a year the taxpayers lay out to process that same paper once it is in the hands of the bureaucracy. None of my fellow businessmen will be surprised to learn that the National Archives estimates that there are over one million forms currently in use by federal agencies. In fact, says the *Wall Street Journal*, the federal bureaucracy each year generates over fifty pages of records for every man, woman, and child in the country. Some 250,000 federal workers now do nothing but file forms and papers into the two million filing cabinets maintained by the Executive branch of government. Those cabinets cover 25 million cubic feet of floor space — twelve times the rentable floor space of the 102-story Empire State building.

All this costs money. According to the Tax Foundation, total spending by the federal government over the fifty-year period of 1922 to 1972 jumped from $3.8 billion to $248 billion. For fiscal 1974, federal spending will bound upward by another $20 billion for an increase of 8.2 percent in *one* year. The fact is that the federal government alone, in fiscal 1974, will take an estimated 25.6 percent of everything we Americans make. And this does not include the 15 percent of our income that will be taken in taxes and spent by state and local bureaucrats.

And the situation is getting worse as control is piled upon control and bureaucracy upon bureaucracy. Consider two typical examples.

In the decade after the regulations of the new Environmental Protection Agency take full effect, for instance, anti-pollution controls for automobiles alone will siphon $95 billion from the pockets of American consumers — a sum greater than the worth of all goods and services produced in Canada for one year, and three times the annual total production of Mexico. The ten-year outlay to be demanded of business and the taxpayers to "clean up the environment" in conformity with new bureaucratic standards is estimated at $287.1 billion — a sum more than five times our total military budget for 1974. Businesses are already strangling in such costs — with many, including a number of manufacturers of badly needed paper, being forced to shut their doors — and there is no evidence that this outlay will do the job.

Equally outrageous is the Occupational Safety and Health Administration, which has unconstitutionally assumed virtually unlimited rights of entry and inspection of every place of business in the country. A policeman may not be able to search the home of a murderer without a warrant, but an OSHAcrat may enter your place of business whenever he likes — and anyone who warns an employer that the man from OSHA is on the way is subject to a $1,000 fine and six months in jail. Thousands of employers have been fined millions of dollars for violations of incredible rules hidden away in the *Federal Register* and bureaucratic archives. In fact, when Senator Carl Curtis went to the Library of Congress to obtain a copy of the OSHA rules, regulations, and appended documents, he was told that he was asking for a pile of papers in excess of 30 feet in height — and that the Library could not check them out even to a U.S. Senator because copies of some of the OSHA regulations were so hard to obtain that it couldn't afford to lose a single copy. Yet, with the OSHA bureaucrats acting as accuser, judge, and jury, American businessmen may be fined $1,000 a day for violating any one of those very regulations!

There are, unfortunately, many scores of EPA's and OSHA's harassing productive Americans in countless ways. Our economy and our liberty are under the gun. And, if it continues, who can doubt that the business end of government will soon deliver the *coup de grâce*?

I urge you to get involved. I know that if enough of you will help, this book can have a powerful educational impact. Often my friends in business, exasperated and distraught at what is happening, declare that they have given up hope of stopping Big Government. Men who ten years ago couldn't even see the problem now shake their heads and wonder if it is too late to save our system of free enterprise. I believe that if we can alert enough Americans to WHAT is happening we will gain the time we need to tell them WHY it is happening. Mr. Smoot's book provides more hard detail on the WHAT of our peril than I have ever before seen between two covers. It is exactly the tool we businessmen have needed to alert our friends, suppliers, customers, and employees. I urge you as strongly as I know how to help get the message of *The*

Business End of Government to everyone you know. Here at last is something you can do that will really count.

Wm. J. Grede
Vice-Chairman, Grede Foundries, Inc.
Past President, National Association of Manufacturers

"There has been a feeling that, in America, it is simply impossible to kill or even slow down the industrial goose that lays the golden eggs . . . . But, today, the goose may well be in the oven . . . . "

Chapter One

Railroading The Public

CALVIN COOLIDGE once said that the business of America is business. He was right. Yet through a large part of our history there have been recurring periods of broad concern with protecting the people against business.

The only effective instrumentality for protecting the public against harmful business practices is a free-market system in which the consumer is king. By exercising free choice to buy or not to buy, consumers can compel businesses to do what a preponderance of consumers want done. When the job of protecting consumers is turned over to government, consumers are dethroned. Government decides what they shall be permitted to buy and at what price and under what conditions. The result is always more harmful to the public than the business practices from which government promised to protect them. Every consumer-protection movement in American history has moved the nation in the wrong direction, has done the opposite of what it promised, has diminished the freedom of the people while augmenting government's oppressive power.

America's first major consumer-protection

movement produced the Interstate Commerce Act of February 4, 1887. This law created the Interstate Commerce Commission (ICC) as an independent executive agency to regulate railroads. Much rhetoric in favor of the ICC law was voiced by reformers and politicians who called the railroads coercive private monopolies, and accused them of bribing or intimidating government officials, of charging the public outrageous rates, of paying low wages, of rendering inferior service, of discriminating against certain industries or geographical areas while favoring others.

These accusations against the railroad interests were generally true, but the label "private monopolies" was inaccurate. It is quite impossible for a truly private enterprise of any kind to acquire such power over any segment of the national economy. Monopolies can come into existence, and survive, only when supported by the force of government. The offending railroads of the Nineteenth Century were built with government subsidies, and they operated under laws (both federal and state) which gave them special privileges. Their undesirable practices were not products of the free-enterprise system. They were created by government. And the ICC remedy was further curtailment by government of the free-enterprise system.

The Interstate Commerce Act did not break up the railroad monopoly. The monopoly disintegrated under the assaults of competition. Even with its government-granted special privileges, the railroad monopoly was already dying before the consumer-protection propaganda for government to control it was ever begun. The big profits being made in railroading encouraged accumulation of private capital to build competing lines, especially in areas where established railroads were most abusive. The railroads tried to form private cartel agreements among themselves to prevent rate-cutting and other bothersome competitive practices. But always there was some maverick who thought he could improve his lot by breaking out of the cartel and getting a larger share of the market by reducing rates and providing the public with superior service.

Unable to maintain their government-granted monopoly, the powerful railroad interests turned to government to do the regulating and price-fixing which they were unable to do themselves. In fact, the pressure that induced Congress to enact the Interstate Commerce Act of 1887 did not come from reformers bemoaning abuses by the powerful railroad interests; it came from the railroad interests themselves, asking Congress to shield them against the harsh winds of competition.

The Interstate Commerce Commission has tried to do that. Though the popular myth is that it was created to protect the public from rate-gouging by the transportation industry, the ICC has devoted much of its activity to keeping transportation rates up rather than down. At first, the ICC prevented railroads from cutting rates and forced all railroads to charge the same, holding that rate-cutting created destructive competition and caused chaos in the industry. Thus the consumers, who were being "protected" from the railroads, were denied the lower prices and better services that some railroads wanted to provide. The established railroads, thus protected, were satisfied — for a while.

Eventually, the development of rival modes of transport (barge lines, trucks and buses, pipelines, airlines) made transportation a keenly competitive industry. It was then that the railroads began to pay a heavy price for having been sheltered by government from competition among themselves. They had lost the resilience and inventiveness necessary to react quickly and creatively in a sharply competitive market. In fact, the regulated railroads, in their cumbersome and ponderous administrative procedures, had come to operate much like government regulatory agencies. There was monumental mismanagement of railroads — encouraged, if not actually fostered, by government.

Moreover, the railroads were now saddled with heavy costs imposed, directly and indirectly, by government. They were forced by the ICC to continue services that occasioned heavy losses. The federal Railway Labor Act of 1926 gave monopolistic control of the railroads' operating employees to the unions; and the unions used their monopolistic power to impose upon railroads high labor costs, low labor productivity, and occasional crippling strikes.

Operating under such burdens, and prohibited

from cutting rates to match those offered by trucks and barge lines, railroads could not effectively compete. In 1900, about 90 percent of all intercity freight was hauled by railroads; in 1950, about 60 percent; in 1970, only about 40 percent.

Occasionally, railroads applied ingenuity and innovation to bring down costs so that they could offer better rates to the public and thus get more business. For example, in the early 1960's, Southern Railway invested $13 million in 500 Big John hopper cars, each of which would carry 90 tons of grain. This increase in hauling capacity so dramatically reduced costs that Southern Railway asked permission to reduce by 60 percent its rates on multiple-car grain shipments. Truckers and barge line operators objected, and the ICC refused Southern's request.

Within a short time after the close of World War II, private automobiles, buses, and airlines had captured most of the long-haul travel business from railroads. Nonetheless the ICC forced railroads to continue running long-haul passenger trains at losses totalling millions of dollars a year.

On October 30, 1970, President Nixon signed the Rail Passenger Service Act setting up Railpax (later called Amtrak), authorizing use of federal tax money to finance a corporation to operate a nationwide railroad passenger system. The public was assailed by much rhetoric about this law; they were assured that it would provide the

American people with the kind of rail travel Americans want and deserve. The actual purpose of the law, however, was to let railroad companies do what the ICC would not permit — that is, divest themselves of unprofitable passenger-train operations. The law allows railroads, if they wish, to transfer all of their intercity passenger operations (except commuter trains) to the new tax-financed corporation.

That was a great relief for many railroads, but it did not come soon enough for all. On June 22, 1971, the nation's biggest railroad — Penn Central, with assets estimated at $6 billion — formally declared itself bankrupt. On December 10, 1971, Congress authorized a 13.5 percent pay raise for railroad workers. Five days later, trustees of the bankrupt Penn Central told a Congressional Subcommittee that the railroad would need $61 million between then and March 1, 1972, just to meet the pay raise ordered by Congress. The trustees said they would be obliged to shut down all Penn Central operations within 45 days if they did not get the money. Congress responded with the Emergency Rail Services Act of 1971, authorizing government guarantees of loans up to $125 million to any railroad undergoing reorganization under the Bankruptcy Act. An entire industry had been crippled because of the government controls it had itself invited years before.

The story of other modes of transport is not identical with that of railroads, but it is somewhat comparable.

Interstate truck lines came under the control of the Interstate Commerce Commission in the late 1930's, because trucking firms asked for it. They could not control price-cutters among themselves — the maverick firms which wanted to get more business by giving the public lower rates — so they asked government to do it for them and government was glad to oblige. Now the ICC will "decertify" or "delicense" a trucking firm for interstate commerce operations if it tries to cut prices or otherwise engage in practices that the ICC regards as "destructive competition."

Big trucking firms that operate in interstate commerce are tightly controlled by the ICC. Complying with ICC regulations is a heavy load on them, but there are compensations. The ICC protects their long-haul business against competition from small trucking firms. It does not take a huge outlay of capital to start a trucking firm, as it does to start a railroad. Hence, there are thousands of small entrepreneurs in the trucking business. But not many of them are ever allowed to grow into big businesses operating across state lines in competition with already established ICC-regulated firms. Truckers cannot operate legally in interstate commerce without ICC certification — which is not easy to get. One case in point:

Joe Jones Jr., a disabled Negro veteran with a family of ten children, had a little trucking business in Atlanta. In 1966, the Small Business Administration lent Jones $25,000 to help him buy a big truck to handle long-haul jobs. Jones bought the truck and contracted for some cargoes; but the Interstate Commerce Commission would not give him a permit to haul across state lines in competition with the firms it was "protecting" by regulation. After making seven fruitless appeals to the bureaucracy for a common-sense ruling, Jones said: "I've been pushed to the verge of bankruptcy, because the government encouraged me to buy expensive equipment so I could help myself, and now they won't let me use it."

Entrepreneur Joe Jones suffered, but so did the consumers who would have benefitted from the lower trucking prices he was willing to work hard hours to provide.

Then there are the airlines, which have been under government subsidies and government regulations from the beginning. In the 1930's, the airlines became disappointed with ICC regulation — in part because there was not enough of it to suit them; there was still too much "destructive competition" among airlines, and not enough tax-subsidization (through mail contracts and otherwise). The result was that Congress passed the Civil Aeronautics Act of 1938, creating the Civil Aeronautics Board (CAB), a special regulatory agency for airlines. The CAB is the absolute czar of the air-transport industry. It fixes rates for air travel and air freight, and determines which airlines may operate in interstate commerce, and on what routes. It is also in charge of dispensing subsidies of tax money to airlines.

The Civil Aeronautics Board began its career by freezing competition in the air-transport industry exactly where it was when CAB took control. When the CAB was created, there were nineteen operating domestic trunk line carriers (airlines operating long hauls in interstate commerce). The CAB certified them all as authorized interstate carriers, and has never certified another one since. Not one new domestic trunkline carrier has been permitted to enter the field of competition since 1938.

By 1973 the original 19 domestic trunk lines of 1938 had shrunk to 11: American, Braniff, Continental, Delta, Eastern, National, Northeast, Northwest, TWA, United, and Western. Most of the shrinkage resulted from weak airlines merging with stronger ones — with CAB approval, of course.

The ingenuity and aggressiveness of private enterprise were, of course, applied to bring competitiveness into the air-transport business and give the public lower rates — despite a Civil Aeronautics Board which is dedicated to maintaining a monopoly for the certified trunk lines and to keeping rates high enough to avoid "destructive competition" in the industry. One major competitive threat to the certified trunk lines came from nonscheduled airlines — firms which were exempt from controls by CAB, under the 1938 law, because they did not operate as common carriers in the sense that they offered regularly scheduled flights. That is, when they could get a profitable load (of cargo or passengers or both) for a particular flight, they would make the flight, at rates below what the trunk lines charged. The "nonskeds" became so popular because of their low rates that they were soon running what almost amounted to regular route service on long hauls, thus cutting into the business of the regulated trunk lines.

The trunk lines were quick to complain. They brought pressure on CAB until, in 1947, the CAB responded by deciding it had authority to require nonscheduled airlines to register with the Board. With registration came regulation, and the CAB rather quickly regulated the nonskeds out of serious competition with regular airlines. In 1949, when CAB asserted full regulatory control over non-scheduled airlines, there were about 150 such firms — offering good, safe service to the public at lower prices than the scheduled airlines offered. Today, there are fewer than 12 such firms; and CAB so circumscribes what they can do that they no longer offer the general public any real alternative to doing business with the officially approved airlines.

Another competitive threat to the CAB-protected airlines came from small feeder airlines, serving communities the big trunk lines could not profitably serve. Most feeders originated as small, tax-subsidized businesses, under CAB control because their operations crossed state lines. The CAB certifies them, and, from time to time, gives one of them "operating rights" over certain short routes that were previously assigned to one of the majors. But the CAB is careful not to let the feeders grow into a real competitive threat to the 11 approved trunk lines. Note, for example, the following from a CAB decision in the *Bonanza-TWA Route Transfer* case of 1949:

"We would like to emphasize again that we have neither the disposition nor the intention to permit local air carriers to metamorphose into trunk lines competitive with the permanently certificated trunk lines. The local service carriers were certificated by us as an experimental effort to bring useful air transporation services into the smaller communities and the isolated or sparsely populated areas of this country and to feed connecting traffic to long-haul carriers. We recognize that some competition between local service carriers and trunk lines is inevitable *but we intend not only to minimize such competition but to prevent its development to the greatest feasible extent.*" (Emphasis added.)

Remember that the stated excuse for the large expenditure of tax money that goes into this regulating of airlines is that the regulation will protect the public. Its real purpose, however, is to protect certain airlines at the expense of the public. (*Note:* Recently, there was some troublesome rate-cutting on the lucrative airline route from California to Hawaii. It was not airline passengers or any other segment of the consuming public which successfully petitioned the CAB to put a stop to this lowering of prices – it was United Airlines.)

11

The CAB certification for an airline to service profitable routes can be worth millions of dollars to the airline that gets the certification. Of course CAB claims to be guided by "public interest" considerations in granting certifications; but that is obviously not so. How can the public interest be better served by granting a valuable certification to Braniff rather than to American, or to American rather than to Eastern? Actually, in making major economic decisions for airlines, the CAB is guided by the caprice or prejudices of a majority of its own members, or by political pressures that often have overtones of bribery and corruption (or, if you prefer, of selfish personal favoritism) at the highest levels of government. Consider two actual cases.

Northeast Airlines first began operating its New York-to-Florida run under temporary CAB certification. After firmly establishing itself on this, its most lucrative route, Northeast applied for permanent certification. In August 1963, the CAB (in a 3-to-2 decision) denied the permanent certification, ordering Northeast to cease its New York-to-Florida service by November fifteenth. The Kennedy family (Robert Kennedy, as Attorney General; Edward Kennedy, as United States Senator) joined forces with other New England politicians and interests, exerting intense pressure on CAB to give Northeast permanent certification. Thus encouraged by the Kennedys and other powerful figures, Northeast continued its New York-to-Florida run in defiance of CAB orders. Eventually, the pressures for Northeast triumphed. In March 1967, CAB reversed itself and granted permanent certification to Northeast for the East Coast run.

In 1968, Braniff was in competition with other major airlines for CAB certification to extend services over certain Pacific routes. Braniff especially wanted permission to open a route to Hawaii via Mexico City and Acapulco. After extensive hearings, a CAB examiner decided that Braniff should not be certified for any of the Pacific routes under consideration.

This CAB decision affected Troy V. Post — a wealthy Dallas man, who was an old friend of President Lyndon B. Johnson and for years had been a heavy contributor to Johnson's political campaigns. Post had been a major stockholder in the holding company that owned Braniff. More than that, however, he was a partner in a 19-million-dollar hotel in Acapulco and was constructing a six-mile beach front and golf course in that resort city. It was financially important to him to have Braniff offering regular flights into Acapulco from Hawaii, the mainland states, and Mexico City.

Post's old friend Lyndon Johnson had another old friend who, thanks to Johnson, was chairman of the CAB. Johnson and his old friend the CAB chairman overruled the CAB examiner and granted Braniff a permit to open a new route from mainland United States to Hawaii via Mexico City and Acapulco. Whatever satisfaction this may have given to Braniff and to Troy Post was short-lived. In 1969, President

Nixon cancelled the CAB certification to Braniff as being "economically unjustified." It was Big Politics as usual.

Meanwhile, just as with railroads and trucking, government regulation is escalating to smother the giant airline interests to which it has granted special privileges. Getting a CAB ruling on proposed price changes for airline tickets takes, on an average, somewhat more than nine months. Getting CAB rulings on such matters as route certification and subsidies takes much longer.

Almost the entire shipping industry is equally victimized. Getting a ruling from the ICC (which regulates railroads, trucks, buses, some barge lines, and other shipping on internal waters) takes an average of eight months, although there have been ICC cases that dragged on for four years before the businesses involved could get rulings clarifying what they could or could not do. The Maritime Commission regulates international oceanic shipping by United States firms. Getting a ruling from the Maritime Commission takes an average of 18 months. The Federal Power Commission (FPC) regulates (among other things) interstate pipeline transportation of natural gas and interstate transmission of electrical power. The FPC is so bogged down in cases that businesses it regulates have had to wait as long as ten years for a final ruling on what they could do.

One small segment of the transportation industry still remains unregulated by the federal government. The consequences of that fact are extremely interesting and significant. Consider:

One of the airlines serving consumers in California is Pacific Southwest Airlines (PSA). Operating solely within that state, PSA is beyond the reach of the federal CAB. Because of a quirk in California law, it can also cut prices without being overruled by the California Public Utility Commission. Never having taken a tax subsidy of any kind (not even mail contracts), PSA is not under the thumb of any government agency. Hence, it operates as a free enterprise.

And what is the result? Competing with three regulated and protected giants — TWA, United, and Western — "little PSA" carries about as many intrastate passengers as all three of them combined. It has an excellent safety record. It provides frequent flights (originating about one thousand flights a week). It uses high-grade equipment. It provides fast, efficient, attractive service that none of the majors match — and at prices which are about one-half of what passengers pay for comparable flights on the East Coast, where there is no unregulated, free-enterprise airline to give service and bring down prices. The majors on the West Coast have complained about PSA's price-cutting, and CAB has allowed them some rate reductions.

The PSA story has a moral. It is that if we would abolish all federal regulatory agencies and allow the forces of free competition to regulate the transportation industry, everyone concerned — the industry, the public, the nation — would be far better off.

Chapter Two

Trustbusting

TRUSTBUSTING was one name given to the consumerism movement of the late Nineteenth Century. It helped to produce not only the Interstate Commerce Act of 1887, but also the Sherman Antitrust Act, which became law on July 2, 1890. Whereas the Interstate Commerce Act created the Interstate Commerce Commission to regulate the railroad "monopoly," the Sherman Antitrust Act undertook to outlaw all monopolies, prohibiting "every contract, combination in the form of trust or otherwise, or conspiracy, in restraint of trade or commerce among the several states, or with foreign nations."

This statute raised impossible problems of interpretation. Without the support or complicity of government, no private business or combination of private businesses could create a monopoly in the sense of prohibiting rival entrepreneurs from entering the same field. Was it illegal restraint of trade for a big business (or a big combination of several businesses) to operate so efficiently that it drove old rivals out of the field and made entry by new rivals difficult? If it was, the law, seeking to prevent restraint of trade, would penalize not only bigness but efficiency, virtually requiring businesses not only to remain small but also not to become too efficient. It would also prohibit the large accumulations of private capital necessary for the industrial development and expansion the nation was then demanding.

Because of this difficulty inherent in the law, the Sherman Antitrust Act for more than 20 years after its enactment did little more than provide an issue for politicians. In 1911, the Supreme Court ruled that business contracts which may be considered somewhat in restraint of trade were not illegal under the Sherman Antitrust Act unless they effected "unreasonable" restraint. That muddied rather than clarified the legal problem, but it sharpened the political issue. Politicians interpreted the Supreme Court decision as soft on big trusts and demanded action. In 1912, Presidential candidate Woodrow Wilson promised to protect the people against big trusts; if the people would elect him, he would plug the loopholes in the Sherman Act. The result, in the second year of Wilson's first term, was the Federal Trade Commission Act and the Clayton Act, both of which were enacted in 1914.

The Federal Trade Commission Act created the Federal Trade Commission (FTC), an independent federal agency (patterned after the first such agency, the ICC), composed of five Presidential appointees with power to investigate corporations alleged to be violating the antitrust laws, and to establish and enforce rules for what a majority of the commissioners deemed to be fair competition in interstate business activities. The FTC Act did not clarify the problem of legal interpretation of antitrust laws, but it did simplify enforcement problems. The five FTC commissioners, by majority vote, could make their own definitions of what was fair and what was unfair, what was in restraint of interstate trade and what was not. They could make their own rules for businesses to obey, investigate alleged violations of their own rules, and then (if they found violations) act as a court to prescribe punishment. It was not constitutional, but it was convenient, and it gave every politician who supported it a claim he could lay before his constituents when pleading for their votes: that he had acted to protect them against the rapacious practices of big business.

The Clayton Act of 1914 attempted to outlaw various business practices which Congress considered as "lessening competition" in interstate commerce. The law restricted business mergers — to the extent of prohibiting one company from buying stock in another company, *if* the purchase caused any "real diminution of competition between the companies." But some of the practices which Congress outlawed as "lessening competition" (price-cutting for certain customers, for example) are in fact very competitive. And the Clayton Act did not simplify the legal problems of interpreting and enforcing antitrust laws. In fact, only one major provision of the law was very clear, very specific, and profoundly important. The Act reflected the growing political power of organized unions. Under the Sherman Antitrust Act, certain union practices had been declared monopolistic and, therefore, illegal. The Clayton Act categorically exempted unions from coverage by federal antitrust laws.

Since 1914, Congress has granted many other special exemptions from federal antitrust laws: export businesses, farmers' cooperatives, insurance, shipping, fishing, communications, electric power – to name but a few.

In 1933, Congress passed Franklin D. Roosevelt's National Industrial Recovery Act, creating the National Recovery Administration (NRA). One purpose of this Act was to force all major American businesses into gigantic cartels or trusts under government control (like the big businesses then operating in Nazi Germany). The NRA directly contradicted the announced purposes of all federal antitrust laws. Consequently, President Roosevelt suspended enforcement of the antitrust laws. Resisting efforts to force them into government-controlled trusts, American businessmen challenged the NRA in federal courts. In 1935, the Supreme Court declared the Act unconstitutional. Angered by business opposition to his NRA, Roosevelt retaliated with vigorous prosecution of businesses under the antitrust laws he had previously suspended; and he demanded more such laws.

The major antitrust law passed during Roosevelt's New Deal Administration was the Robinson-Patman Act of 1936. Though broad in scope, this Act was aimed primarily at chain stores; it was intended to keep them from giving the public such low prices that big chains would be "unfair" competition for small stores. Several state governments enacted their own versions of the Robinson-Patman Act. These are generally referred to as state Fair Trade Laws.

Robinson-Patman further added to the welter of complications and contradictions involved in government efforts to regulate business "for the benefit of the public." For if, on the one hand, you are a manufacturer who makes an agreement with competing manufacturers that you will sell a certain product for a certain price to a certain type of distributor, you violate the Sherman Act of 1890, as amended; the Clayton Act of 1914, as amended; and probably the Federal Trade Commission Act of 1914. But on the other hand, if you *do not* sell that certain product for a certain price to a certain type of distributor, you violate the Robinson-Patman Act of 1936, and probably the Fair Trade Laws of a dozen or more states.

The ostensible purpose of all these laws is to help the public. The assumption behind this purpose is that if merchants are left alone, they will all get together and raise prices and thus overcharge consumers for everything. In practice, however, the laws *require merchants to keep prices high*. There have been many more cases against business for charging low prices than for charging high prices.

In 1950, Congress enacted the Celler-Kefauver Antimerger Act to broaden, clarify, and strengthen the antimerger provisions of the old Clayton Act. Like all the antitrust laws which preceded it, Celler-Kefauver did not clarify, but further thickened, the nebulous confusion which enshrouds governmental antitrust programs. For the past 20 years (since enactment of the Celler-Kefauver Antimerger Act), the bulk of the federal government's antitrust activity has been focused on controlling business mergers. This is true even though the government has no valid, constitutional authority to prohibit one business firm from buying out another, any more than it has authority to prohibit a dairy farmer from buying his neighbor's cows.

What criteria do federal administrators use to determine that one business merger is good, another bad? Why would the Civil Aeronautics Board determine that United Airlines' acquisition of Capitol Airlines was good and permissible, as it did in 1961, but later determine that a merger of Eastern and American and a merger of TWA and Pan American were bad and impermissible?

In 1963, the FTC and the Department of Justice allowed Gulf Oil Company to purchase Midway Coal Company. In 1966, they permitted Continental Oil Company to buy Consolidation Coal Company (one of the two largest coal-producing companies). In 1971, however, they decided that Kennecott Copper Company's purchase of Peabody Coal Company was a violation of the Clayton Act because it "substantially lessened competition in the U.S. coal industry." Why?

At a time when a basic American industry — steel — is being driven to the wall by competition with lower-cost production by foreign mills, the Department of Justice prohibits a merger of Bethlehem Steel and Youngstown Sheet and Tube, thus foreclosing the possibility of greater efficiency and lower prices that the merger could have achieved — and prohibiting also the large pooling of private capital which the American steel industry needs in order to compete with foreign producers, many of whom are subsidized by their governments. Why?

There is no reasonable answer to these questions. A business merger is either good or bad, *as the thinking of government administrators makes it so*.

Clearly, the federal antitrust statutes are not a body of laws that can be impartially interpreted and universally enforced for all covered businesses. They are discretionary laws, applied or not applied at the discretion of enforcement officials. Discretionary laws are always potentially blackmail or blackjack laws, which breed bribery and corruption. Congress should repeal them all. Stop the federal government's unconstitutional meddling in the marketplace, and no combination of private business interests could ever create a lasting monopoly damaging to the public.

Chapter Three

Unions And Labor Laws

OF THE MANY federal laws which can be characterized as descendants of the old Interstate Commerce Act and the Sherman Antitrust Act, none have done more damage than federal labor laws.

There is irony in this. Two laws enacted in the Nineteenth Century to protect the public against combines of business wealth have helped to bring on other laws that have created other combines of privately controlled wealth (in the big labor unions) far more damaging to society than business ever was or could have been.

In mid-1971, Harry Bridges, an old-line Communist, called out his International Longshoremen's and Warehousemen's Union on a strike that lasted until February 19, 1972, closing all U.S. Pacific ports, including those in Hawaii and Alaska. For a while, some goods moved in and out of the United States through Canadian and Mexican ports, but Bridges quickly plugged those loopholes. In testimony before a Congressional committee, he warned the Congress not to interfere with his strike, threatening to call on his "friends in other countries" to tie up American ships in foreign ports.

The strike did enormous economic damage, not just to shipping interests, but to the entire nation: to farmers, laborers, investors, bankers, manufacturers, trucking firms, railroads, and consumers — which means everyone. Bridges was indifferent about it all. He argued that it *takes* a lot of damage to win union demands. During the strike, President Nixon ordered a wage-price freeze which would make it illegal for businesses to grant the kind of wage increases Bridges was after. Harry Bridges said: "We are telling Uncle Sam either he approves our settlement when we reach it or those lousy ships will stay tied up." How long? "Until all the damn money in the settlement is assured," he said.

No top leader in the Executive branch of government, in the Congress, or in either of the major political parties spoke publicly a word of criticism of Harry Bridges.

In late July 1971, the Bell Telephone Company ended a nationwide strike by granting union demands for a 31 percent pay raise, at a time when inflation was already a harrowing national problem. But a 31 percent raise was not enough for union bosses of New York locals. They kept workers out on strike well into 1972. During that time there were many criminal acts of violence against company property — acts that went unpunished.

Events like those of 1971 and 1972 have been routine for a long time. No business firm, however large, can successfully resist a big union's demands, however unjustified and extortionate. And the problem is growing worse. Nowadays, for example, the federal government forces taxpayers to subsidize strikes — by giving food stamps (totalling millions of dollars a year) to people who are "unemployed" because they are on strike.

Having learned that resisting union demands is as futile as it is costly, some of the biggest businesses do not seriously try any more: they just give in to the demands, eventually passing the cost on (as they must) to the general public. In late July 1971, the steel industry avoided a strike that would have damaged the country as much as did Harry Bridges' strike, by granting union demands for a 31 percent pay raise *plus an unlimited ceiling on cost-of-living adjustments.*

What this means in practical terms is most interesting. The National Commission on Food Marketing, established by the federal government, made a two-year study of the distribution of food from farmer to consumer. In 1966 the Commission released an 11-volume report on its findings. One item will serve to illustrate them: It costs about as much to deliver a loaf of bread from the bakery to the consumer as it does to grow the wheat, mill the flour, and bake the bread — because of labor costs. The editor of that report was James E. Roper, a free-lance writer. Later, Mr. Roper wrote an article on "Why Food Prices Keep Rising," which was published in the January 1973 issue of *Reader's Digest.* The headnote to the article sums it up rather well:

"Labor unions involved in food distribution have made a fine art of featherbedding, make-work and greed. Until they agree to provide a day's work for a day's pay, housewives will continue to find 'hidden costs' at the checkout counter."

Three powerful unions are involved in food distribution: the Teamsters, whose members haul merchandise to stores; the Retail Clerks International Association, which represents all employees in unionized stores except meat workers; and the Amalgamated Meat Cutters and Butcher Workmen of North America. Each has its own featherbedding and make-work rackets, which it forces upon the various managements involved. One example: Because of a Teamsters' Union requirement that sales commissions be paid to drivers who deliver trailerloads of bread or milk (although the drivers do no selling), one truckdriver in Los Angeles collected, in 16 months, $104,000 in sales commissions, in addition to his regular salary.

Not all union activity is devoted to getting benefits for union members. The essential motivation for union activity is to get dues-paying members for the unions and to keep union bosses secure in their plush and powerful jobs, which grow more plush and more powerful as union membership grows. In *Union Power and The Public Interest*, by Dr. Emerson P. Schmidt (published in 1973), a man who had worked in the coal fields as a union organizer for the United Mine Workers is quoted as saying: "We had men who went in with a stick of dynamite in one hand and a shotgun in the other. They just terrorized people into paying royalties and into joining the union."

How did unions acquire such power? The federal government gave it to them. The unions have enormous financial resources because the federal government exempts them from paying taxes on their billion-dollar-plus annual income from compulsory membership dues. Unions use their wealth (in violation of the tax code that gives them tax exemption, and in violation of federal labor laws that guarantee their existence) to campaign for politicians who support unions; and they are remarkably effective.

In the 1970 Congressional elections, AFL-CIO's COPE (Committee on Political Education) endorsed 361 candidates for Congress, of whom 219 (61 percent) were elected. As *Congressional Quarterly* put it: "Organized labor scored notable successes at the polls in November [1970], particularly in connection with Congressional committee assignments dealing with labor questions." In 1972, according to labor columnist Victor Riesel, unions spent $50 million in their "drive to elect George McGovern and a friendly, liberal, controllable Congress."

The unions play politics because it is politics that assures their special privileges. The basic federal labor law is the National Labor Relations Act of 1935. It was amended by the Taft-Hartley Act of 1947, and by the Landrum-Griffin Act of 1959. As administered by the

National Labor Relations Board (NLRB), with the support of federal courts, these laws have given unions monopolistic control over a significant segment of the labor force in the United States. Without such laws, compulsory unionism could not exist.

Even with the special government-granted privileges and power it has enjoyed for 38 years, compulsory unionism has failed to achieve its goal of capturing the total labor force of the United States. The majority of workers in this country are still not union members. To make progress in recruiting new members — or even to hold those they have — the unions must use coercive tactics sanctioned by federal law. Union bosses tacitly admit as much. This is why they oppose Right-to-Work laws which allow workers the freedom to join, or not to join, a union as they please.

There are many cases which show the pro-union bias, and the anti-workingman and anti-business bias, of federal labor laws. The classic, perhaps, is the Kohler case.

In the early 1950's, Walter Reuther (now deceased, then head of United Auto Workers) spent many months and much money trying to organize the Kohler Company of Kohler, Wisconsin, by persuading a majority of Kohler employees to join the union. Some joined, but most refused. Reuther demanded that management sign a contract that would force the employees to join his union. Management refused. It did not discriminate against employees who freely chose to join the union, but it would not compel others to join. On April 5, 1954, Reuther's organizers started a strike to bludgeon the company into forcing union membership on its employees. The union massed imported pickets at the gates of the plant, and instituted a train of violence that resulted in murder, vandalism, arson, boycott, and terrorism against innocent people. The violence and terror were not confined to the plant and its immediate environs. They engulfed the whole town and the surrounding community.

On August 26, 1960, the NLRB ruled against Kohler and in favor of the United Auto Workers on most issues in the six-year-old strike, ordering Kohler to reinstate nearly all strikers. Subsequently, a U.S. Court of Appeals upheld the 1960 NLRB ruling, but asked the Board to review the cases of some striking workers who had not been rehired. On September 29, 1964, the NLRB ordered Kohler to offer jobs, with payment of wages back to January 1962, to 57 strikers not covered by the 1960 NLRB ruling — even though they had been guilty of violence and intimidation against non-striking employees.

On December 17, 1965, Kohler Company officials accepted a one-year contract with the union, agreeing to pay $3 million in back wages to strikers and to contribute $1.5 million to restore their pension rights. All told (according to estimates of UAW union officials), the strike cost Kohler between $25 million and $35 million.

Union bosses used to call the Taft-Hartley Act "the slave labor law." Maybe they were right.

Chapter Four

The Fourth Branch: Regulation

JUDGED BY their accomplishments, the two major Nineteenth Century laws to protect the public against business — the Interstate Commerce Act of 1887 and the Sherman Antitrust Act of 1890 — have been failures. They have not achieved lower prices and better business services for the public, but have made matters worse. Judged by their impact on constitutional government in the United States, the two old laws can be characterized as calamities.

Constitutional authority for both laws rests on one provision of the Constitution giving Congress power to regulate interstate commerce. That provision was intended to keep state governments from erecting barriers (tariffs, quotas, embargoes, and so on) to the free flow of trade across state lines. It was not intended to empower the federal government to dominate such trade or to interfere with private business activities. But Presidents, Congresses, and federal courts have stretched all meaning out of the phrase *interstate commerce*. With the Interstate Commerce Act of 1887 and the Sherman Act of 1890 as basic authorization for hundreds of other laws, the federal government now exercises autocratic control over myriad economic activities.

Since President Franklin D. Roosevelt succeeded in packing the U.S. Supreme Court with New Deal justices, the Court in a series of rulings (beginning with *National Labor Relations Board v. Jones-Laughlin Steel Company*, 1937) has held that Congress can do anything it pleases to regulate commerce in the United States — even local trade, if Congress alleges that it will affect interstate commerce. Where matters of federal regulation of commerce are concerned, the Tenth Amendment (which prohibits the federal government from exercising powers not granted to it by the Constitution) has been ruled by the Supreme Court to be mere rhetoric. Elevator operators have been officially declared to be engaged in interstate commerce because they work in buildings that house firms which do business across state lines. Farmers who raise grain to feed their own livestock are said to be engaged in interstate commerce because the grain they raise and feed on their farms may prevent an equivalent amount of grain from moving in interstate commerce.

Moreover, the Interstate Commerce Act of 1887 has been the progenitor of a system of "administrative law" that violates almost every fundamental principle of liberty written into the U.S. Constitution and Bill of Rights. As previously mentioned, the Act created the Interstate Commerce Commission as an independent federal agency to administer its provisions. The agency is called independent because the commissioners who run it are not controlled by anyone. They operate under grants of power made by Congress. They are appointed by the President, but for fixed terms that always exceed the elected term of the President who appoints them. Consequently, it is rare for all members of the Commission to be appointees of one President. This not only makes the Interstate Commerce Commission independent of the President, but also dilutes an incumbent President's accountability to the public for what the Commission does. And of course, because they are not elected, the commissioners are wholly independent of the public.

For 27 years (1887 to 1914), the Interstate Commerce Commission was the only federal independent administrative agency in existence. In 1914, Congress created another one, the Federal Trade Commission, modeled after the ICC. Today we have many such federal agencies. There are also hundreds of federal regulatory or administrative agencies which are not called independent, because they are under the jurisdiction of some executive department (Agriculture, Commerce, Defense, Transportation, HEW, and so on), but their mode of operation is essentially the same as that of the independent agencies. No one really knows how many federal regulatory agencies there are. The number is large.

The Constitution established a federal government of three branches, Legislative, Executive, and Judicial. One fundamental principle guiding and motivating the Founding Fathers who wrote our Constitution was that concentrations of political power are fatal to liberty. Time and again, delegates to the Constitutional Convention of 1787 warned one another that to form a government in which it was possible ever to combine the legislative, executive, and judicial functions in one branch would be to create a more oppressive governmental system than the one the American colonies had rebelled against.

In the regulating agencies all of these powers are now illegally merged. These agencies constitute an unconstitutional fourth branch of the federal government.

Congress makes broad grants of power to the administrative agencies, enabling them to make whatever rules and regulations they may deem necessary to carry out the purposes of the laws they administer and enforce. Their administrative rules and regulations have the force of law; and the administrators can change this "law" any time they wish, without consulting anyone. All they have to do is promulgate a new rule or regulation and publish it in the *Federal Register.* Thirty days after publication, it becomes a binding "law."

The citizens who are bound by this kind of "administrative law" frequently cannot find out what it is. The *Federal Register* is both difficult to obtain and expensive. Administrative laws published in the *Register* are also hard to understand, unless you are a trained and experienced lawyer. Even if you could understand them, you would have to spend most of your time reading the *Federal Register* just to keep up with the thousands of new and changed administrative laws published in it. The complexity of the administrative laws that fill the *Register* is so vast and contradictory that no one knows what is required of the citizens who are bound by them. This body of law is superimposed on the normal complex of laws enacted by Congress; and it controls most economic activity in the United States.

What happens when a taxpayer runs afoul of an administrative law? The agency that exercised legislative power in making the law exercises executive power to investigate violations of it and to enforce it. When investigating alleged violations of its own regulations, a federal regulatory agency is not bound by constitutional provisions that restrict the police in their investigations under statutory law. Inspectors or examiners for a regulatory agency may enter private premises and make searches without specifying what they are looking for and without search warrants. If the taxpayer resists, the inspectors do not obtain a valid search warrant; rather, they seek a court order prohibiting interference with the inspectors. Then, if the taxpayer resists an illegal search − one in violation of the Fourth Amendment − he can be jailed without a trial for contempt of court. After exercising Executive power to investigate violations of its own administrative law, the regulatory agency exercises Judicial power to make findings of guilt and to assess penalties — without due process of law, in violation of the Fifth Amendment; and without a trial by jury, in violation of the Sixth Amendment.

What if the taxpayer feels he has been unjustly treated and wants to appeal the decision made against him by a regulatory agency? He cannot appeal to the federal courts until he has exhausted all "administrative remedies." This means that his first appeal must be made to some arm of the same agency that made the law and found him guilty under it. Generally, the agency upholds itself on this appeal — and the taxpayer loses.

During all these proceedings, the taxpayer's time and energies are being diverted from the pursuits by which he makes a living, while the government employees arrayed against him are doing the nine-to-five jobs which provide them with incomes. Moreover, the taxpayer pays his own legal and other expenses directly, while indirectly (through taxes) helping to pay the expenses and salaries of those who are fighting him with the enormous resources of the federal government. Even among those businessmen who have the courage to try, there are very few who have the money or the time necessary to fight their cases all the way through the labyrinth of administrative bureaucracy to get them into the regular courts. Those few who do often go into court with a heavy prejudice and presumption of guilt against them because they have already been found guilty by several administrative tribunals.

Lowell Mason served on the Federal Trade Commission for 11 years (1945-1956). Throughout that time, his was the voice of dissent. After his retirement from the FTC, Mr. Mason collected his dissents (and some of his concurring opinions) into a volume called *The Language of Dissent* (published in 1959). Concerning his 11-year tenure as a Federal Trade Commissioner, Mason says:

> A sense of loneliness at the Commission encouraged me to get out and speak before as many trade associations as invited me . . . .
>
> As an administrator of two antitrust laws diametrically opposed to each other, it was not difficult for me to accuse everybody at a trade convention with being some kind of a lawbreaker. Either they were all charging everyone the same price, a circumstance indicating a violation of the Sherman Act, or they were *not* charging everyone the same price, a circumstance indicating a violation of the Robinson-Patman Act.
>
> Most businessmen took this kind of jibing in good grace. But at one convention, a man interrupted my speech to say the Commission had recently sued him for doing both. To which I replied:
>
> "Then in that event, how can you win? We shall probably find you guilty of one or the other!"
>
> His retort: "You damn fools found me guilty of both . . . ."

In more serious vein, Lowell Mason writes:

The fight against tyranny in America is dull and monotonous in these years of grace of the mid-Twentieth Century. It consists almost entirely of a lot of petty recognitions of the petty encroachments, arrogances, and cruelties of bureaucracy that lie hidden under the government's sweet promise of security.

This is the modern tyranny of the total state — Western style. It adds up in the end to something considerably more pervasive than the gibbet or the stake of medieval times, but it is much less spectacular than the modern Eastern tyrannies of Katyn Forest or Budapest . . . .

It is not communists or even socialists who can successfully advance tyrannical precedents — they are too unpopular. The real work toward ultimate bureaucratic control is done by innocent zealots of an entirely different hue . . . .

The most effective way peaceful totalitarianism can be achieved in the United States is through complete government control of the common everyday acts of all people — and I do not mean by putting everybody on the government payroll. What field of peacetime activity concerns nearly everybody? Business, trade, and commerce . . . .

Today, a series of administrative court decisions are being quietly built up in the world of commerce which may provide future precedents for tyranny in any phase of a man's life.

Even though administrative courts invade fundamental rights of citizens in a manner no real court would tolerate, when real courts are called upon to review such actions, they merely shrug their judicial shoulders and look the other way . . . .

Actually, there is evolving in the United States the same kind of jurisprudence that exists in the Communist-controlled countries, especially during the period when Communists are solidifying their control. At that stage in particular, Communist governments are relatively tolerant with individuals who commit crimes of violence and moral depravity; but they brutally punish economic and political offenses. It is not common criminals who are sent to slave camps in Siberia, but persons accused of disobeying the economic and political commands of the Communist State.

Similarly, in the United States, as government controls fashion our economy into the likeness of Communism, businessmen who violate the economic commands of regulatory agencies are considered more dangerous than criminals. Our courts and other branches of government are becoming so permissive about crime and so concerned about the rights of criminals that the right of society to be protected is sometimes ignored; but businessmen accused of economic offenses are punished without due process of law.

Lowell Mason makes this point, and illustrates it by telling of a deputy fire marshal in Ohio who sentenced a man to jail after holding a secret inquisitorial proceeding. The defendant was not even allowed to have his own attorney present. The Supreme Court upheld the sentence *because* the trial "was not a criminal trial"; it was "an administrative investigation of incidents damaging to the economy."

Chapter Five

Harassment: The OSHA Syndrome

THE SAME kind of anti-business animus that inspired the federal labor laws and created the NLRB also produced the Occupational Safety and Health Act of 1970 and its creature, OSHA — the Occupational Safety and Health Administration.

An original proponent of OSHA was Ralph Nader, who has been quoted as saying that "what is needed is socialism or communism of one sort or another." In the June 15, 1968 issue of *The New Republic*, there is an article by Ralph Nader and Jerome Gordon arguing for "a comprehensive federal program designed to end colossal inaction and penury by our society in dealing with the following conditions: Every working day 55 workers die, 8500 are disabled and 27,200 are injured . . . ."

In 1968, President Lyndon Johnson proposed an occupational health and safety bill giving the Secretary of Labor authority to set and enforce safety standards for American industry. In 1969, President Nixon asked Congress to establish a National Occupational Safety and Health Board with power to set standards for protecting most of the nation's workers. In 1970, Nader and

Nixon were joined by the most powerful lobby in America — the combined forces of monopolistic unionism.

During House debate on the OSHA bill (November 23 and 24, 1970), Representative Dominick V. Daniels (D.-N.J.) said: "Every day we postpone passage means 55 more American workers will die; 8500 will be disabled, and 27,200 will be injured." Compare Daniels' statement in November 1970 with that of Ralph Nader and Jerome Gordon in June 1968.

This was the core and the quintessence of *all* arguments ever made, by anyone, for the OSHA legislation. There were some variations on the theme, and the statistics were sometimes juggled around a bit; but, in essence, the demand for OSHA rested on one assertion: We must have federal legislation to stop the ghastly slaughter of American workers.

The promise was that federal job-safety legislation would eliminate deaths and injuries being suffered by employees of business. The implication of this promise was that if businesses had done, without federal legislation, all that the legislation would require them to do, there would have been no work-caused illnesses and accidents. The job-safety legislation had no provisions requiring safe behavior by employees or placing any obligation for safety upon them. Obviously, then, the total blame for all deaths and injuries suffered by employees of business was placed exclusively on businessmen.

There is no reason to believe that businessmen, as a group, have less human compassion and social conscience than any other group, including consumer advocates, union bosses, and politicians. Moreover, businessmen have profit-motivated reasons for fostering on-the-job safety. Work-caused injuries and illnesses are costly.

Judged by any objective standard, the on-the-job safety record of American industry is good — and has been improving yearly. Between 1912 and 1971, according to the National Safety Council's *Accident Facts,* 1972 edition, accidental work deaths per 100,000 population were reduced 67 per cent, from 21 to 7. In 1912, an estimated 18,000 to 21,000 workers' lives were lost. In 1971 there were 14,200 work deaths in a work force double in size and producing over seven times as much as that of 1912.

The Occupational Safety and Health Act of 1970 created OSHA, within the Labor Department, as its administrative agency. The Secretary of Labor was authorized to set, through OSHA, "mandatory occupational safety and health standards applicable to businesses affecting interstate commerce." The only exclusions from the law's coverage are government agencies and employers covered by other federal safety-and-health laws (such as the Federal Coal Mine Health and Safety Act of 1969 and the Atomic Energy Act of 1954). By official Labor Department interpretation, the phrase "businesses affecting interstate commerce," as used in the OSHA statute, can mean every person, corporation, partnership, proprietorship, or other entity which hires one or more employees anywhere in the United States, or on the outer continental shelf, or in the nation's territories, possessions, and protectorates. At least 13.5 million employers fall into this broad category. It covers everything.

The bureaucrats of OSHA may never contrive to extend their jurisdiction actively to the limit of the agency's immense potential, but they are trying. In February 1972, when OSHA had just completed its ninth month of operations, the Assistant Secretary of Labor then in charge of the organization said OSHA was endeavoring "to establish ... [its] presence in the field as broadly as possible." He said this was being accomplished by the process OSHA was using in selecting businesses to investigate, since, manifestly, it could not investigate all businesses. He explained the selecting process as making "a random cross section of all kinds of establishments — in all kinds of industries and of all sizes from the largest to the smallest — on as broad a geographical basis as possible."

In its first full fiscal year of operation, OSHA cited employers for 102,860 violations — an average of 8,571 a month. In one month of 1973 (March), OSHA issued more than 18,000 citations.

In the legal enforcement of normal laws, police are not allowed to make a random selection of a man's name, and then raid his place, without a warrant, on the chance that they may find evidence of some violation of some law. Before police can make a legal search, they must get a warrant. Before they can get a warrant, they must show a judge or other magistrate "probable cause" for issuing the warrant (*i.e.*, must present information indicating that the man whose premises are to be searched has committed a specific crime, and must specify the particular evidence they expect to find).

In the enforcement of administrative law, no court orders, warrants, warnings, or administrative notices of intent are required — not even any information about the victim, except that he is an employer. OSHA compliance officers are given unlimited authority "to enter without delay and at reasonable times any ... workplace or environment where work is performed by an employee of an employer; and to inspect and investigate during regular working hours and at other reasonable times."

The compliance officer decides what is "reasonable." The OSHA compliance officers can — and, on occasion, do — shut down a small business while an inspection is being made, although OSHA's own *Compliance Operations Manual* provides that inspections "shall be such as to preclude unreasonable disruption of the operations of the employer's establishment."

Making sudden raids to catch employers by surprise and find them in technical violation of some regulation is a primary OSHA enforcement tactic — authorized, in fact, by the law, which provides penalties of a fine of $1000 and a six-month jail sentence against any person who (without OSHA permission) gives an employer advance notice of an inspection.

The consequences of sudden raids are often painful to employers — like Bill Riddle, who owns the Ace Cabinet Company (Yuma, Arizona), and has four employees. Frayed cords on power tools are continuing hazards in his shop. Therefore, Mr. Riddle (who says, "It would be stupid to hurt a man who is making a living for me") closely watches the tools and changes power cords promptly when needed. In September 1972, an OSHA compliance officer made a surprise call at the Ace Cabinet Company while Mr. Riddle was changing cords on power tools. Riddle had just finished two tools and was about to start on a third, which he showed to the inspector, explaining what he was doing.

The officer cited Riddle for a violation because the tool still had a frayed cord when the officer saw it. That was just the beginning for Riddle. He was ordered to ground an electric box in his shop, but an electrical contractor subsequently told him that grounding the box would be dangerous. Riddle had two expensive saws used for specialized work in cabinet making. The saws were designed without safety guards, and cannot do the work for which they were designed if safety guards are added. He was ordered by OSHA to install safety guards anyway.

It is fixed OSHA policy to punish employers

for employee actions which employers could not possibly prevent. One instance: An employee of the Atlas Roofing Company, working on a building in North Carolina, deliberately removed a safety guard covering a hole in the roof and committed suicide by jumping into the hole. Incredibly, OSHA fined Atlas $500 because the covering was not in place.

When asked why employees have no responsibility for safety under the OSHA statute and under OSHA regulations, one OSHA official (Edward E. Estkowski, administrator of OSHA Region V, Chicago) replied that management wants responsibility for the health and safety of its own employees, and that the federal government does not want to intervene in labor-management relations.

Employers are penalized for violating OSHA requirements which contribute nothing to the safety or health of employees — and even for violating OSHA requirements which make matters worse for employees. Some illustrations:

● Employers are required to color-code certain switches red and green, although they may already have their equipment coded with other colors which employees understand through years of use.

● Farmers must install roll bars on their tractors, even though there are many tractors to which roll bars cannot possibly be attached; even though roll bars cost $200, which in many instances is more than a tractor is worth; and even though, in the major farming region of the

Great Plains, farm tractors are generally driven on level land and flat roads.

● OSHA requires a half-inch protective mesh on *all* motors and power ventilating equipment; but in the poultry business, feathers will completely plug such screens within a few days.

● Characteristically, OSHA compelled the owner of a printing plant to replace more than $300 worth of new toilet seats because they did not have open fronts. He was in violation of Subsection 311 of Section 1910.141 of the OSHA regulations, which declared: "Every water closet shall have a hinged *open front* seat made of substantial material having a nonabsorbent finish." Open-front toilet seats are required because, theoretically, they provide better sanitation; but, in reality, they do not provide it. Regardless of construction, toilet seats cannot be kept sanitary if people use them carelessly.

● On May 16, 1972, OSHA cited the Fountain Foundry Company (Pueblo, Colorado) for an excess of silica dust in the air at the plant, and ordered Fountain to submit an "abatement plan" by June 2. Fountain imported from Chicago a consultant who established that the silica dust came from heavy traffic which local authorities had temporarily detoured onto an unpaved road running past the foundry. Nonetheless, OSHA commanded Fountain to provide dust masks for employees. Employees refused to wear the masks because they are uncomfortable and dangerous: they make breathing difficult;

they induce perspiration which limits vision; they invite eye injuries by impeding the use of safety goggles. In the course of making matters worse at Fountain Foundry, OSHA cost the company more than $100,000.

● OSHA required the Sedona Sheet Metal Company (Sedona, Arizona) to spend some $3,000 to provide an employee lunch room containing 13 square feet of space for each of its 12 employees, who neither needed nor wanted a lunch room.

● And Dan Callahan, a painting contractor in Pennsylvania, tells of an OSHA citation because an old dump truck being used exclusively as a container (never moved from its location) had improper brake lights and a cracked windshield.

Such outrages are, in fact, common. Many OSHA actions against employers reflect a vengeful attitude toward businessmen, while others seem to reflect merely the exasperating silliness of bureaucracy.

The Occupational Safety and Health Administration formally came into existence on April 28, 1971. It hastily compiled some 100,000 safety standards to impose on employers, by incorporating hundreds of "consensus standards" into its own code. "Consensus standards" is jargon, meaning standards that were already in use by various industries; guidelines that had been recommended by federal agencies, trade associations, and union groups; standards required by older federal laws applying to specific industrial activity, and so on.

These "consensus standards" were adopted without any review to determine what they required, how they should be applied, and whether they were adequate or practical. Many of them contradict each other; some are so complex that compliance is impossible; many are patently absurd; some are obsolete. On May 29, 1971, OSHA published them as a 357,000-word set of rules and regulations, which filled 250 pages in the *Federal Register*, and which 30 days after their publication became binding as law on American employers. In June 1972, OSHA issued a booklet containing 17 additional *Federal Register* pages (about 25,000 words) of regulations which had been issued since May 29, 1971.

This adds up to 380,000 words of rules and regulations published by OSHA during the first 11 months of its operation — in addition to booklets and leaflets containing supplementary instructions on record keeping, notice posting, and what not. And there is more. In addition to the regulations it published, OSHA "referenced in" many others — that is, made reference in footnotes to safety codes and regulations not published by OSHA that OSHA enforces on employers. An official of the National Small Business Association estimates that it would cost an employer more than $300 just to buy all the documents needed (in addition to OSHA-published materials) for a complete set of OSHA-enforced regulations. If all 13.5 million employers actually spent $300 each for all the documents they need to find out what OSHA requires of them, the total cost to them would be more than $4 billion.

There is still more. Although primary enforcement responsibility was given to OSHA in the Department of Labor, NIOSH in the Department of Health, Education and Welfare was given responsibility for research, investigation, and experimentation to develop new safety-and-health standards and to devise employee safety-and-health programs. NIOSH is an acronym for the National Institute of Occupational Safety and Health, which the OSHA statute created. The reporting and record keeping that NIOSH requires of employers are in addition to those devised by OSHA. A state may set up its own occupational safety-and-health program. If the program meets OSHA approval, OSHA will withdraw its inspectors from the state, but will still require of employers within the state all the reporting it requires in other states. The state agency must also make frequent reports to OSHA and will be subject to "disapproval" at any time. Both OSHA and NIOSH can make grants to states for experimentation and research concerning safety and health, and OSHA can make grants to pay for 90 percent of the cost of administering and enforcing OSHA-approved state programs.

In February 1972, George C. Guenther, then OSHA director, warned that every American businessman "ought to be familiarizing himself with his responsibilities under the act." To do that, the 13.5 million businessmen potentially covered by the Act would have to spend more than 350 million man-hours of time just reading the rules and regulations that OSHA itself published during its first year.

Of course, OSHA officials generally sneer at such startling statistics. They assert that a businessman obviously needs only to refer to the OSHA standards and rules that apply to his particular industry. In this case, the obvious is not obvious. If single copies of each were put in one pile, the rules, warnings, notices, posters, explanations, clarifications, and other documents issued by OSHA during its first year would make a stack 17 feet high. This material was published without indices or other aids to make it usable as handy reference. Employers are given no specific notices, guides, or instructions about their responsibilities. They must read it all to determine (if they can) what applies to them. If an employer does not take this precaution, an unexpected inspection could find him in violation of requirements he knows nothing about. How, except by reading volumes of OSHA safety regulations, can a television repairman, with one hired helper, know that the clothes hangers and door latches in his toilet must meet prescribed national standards, or find out what those standards are?

If an employer asks OSHA for guidance, he only invites trouble. One small businessman who asked OSHA for help in determining what he was supposed to do to comply with OSHA regulations got this reply: "If a compliance officer visits your place of employment, he is obligated to conduct a complete walk-around inspection. If he finds any alleged violations it could subject you to assessment of monetary penalties. If you still desire a visit under these conditions, please let us know."

American Opinion contributing editor Alan Stang discussed this sticky point with Howard J. Schulte, the OSHA regional administrator in Denver. Stang reports: "I asked how a businessman can ask OSHA for advice, in view of the fact that if he tells OSHA his problem, he may very well be fined. Schulte replied that the employer can 'call up anonymously.' So it is easy to imagine businessmen across the country, wearing dark glasses and with their hat brims pulled low, calling OSHA from coin telephones with handkerchiefs over the mouthpiece."

Obviously, as OSHA officials might say, 13.5 million American employers have not spent, and will not spend, more than 350 million man-hours reading all of OSHA's regulations. Consequently, a big percentage of OSHA penalties against employers are for failure to obey OSHA regulations whose existence had never been suspected by the employers.

The Agnew Lumber Company in Grants Pass, Oregon, was cited for 13 violations of OSHA regulations concerning ladders. For years, Agnew had been using ladders with rungs 14 inches apart; but OSHA says the rungs should be 12 inches apart. Guard rails in the Agnew plant were 36 inches high, as required by Oregon state regulations, and by OSHA itself in some of its regulations; but an OSHA inspector cited Agnew for violations because he found four places in the plant where, he claimed, OSHA regulations required a 42-inch guard rail. Agnew was cited for two "serious violations" involving guards around flat chains, although the guards had been examined and approved by Oregon state inspectors and by Agnew's insurance carrier.

In all, Agnew was cited for 37 violations. Don Deardorf, production manager at Agnew, says that when *any* plywood plant is operating there will be some veneer on the floor somewhere, or a millwright will occasionally lay a torch down momentarily without turning it off; but these are violations of OSHA regulations. The only way the management of a plywood plant can avoid violations of OSHA rules is to shut the plant down.

In fact, with the limitless powers Congress has granted OSHA, with the complex of administrative law OSHA has created, and with the unconstitutional enforcement techniques OSHA uses, OSHA officials could harass all American private businesses out of existence.

Consider, for example, OSHA's power over the construction industry. There is no possibility that OSHA will improve the safety record of this industry; but OSHA will increase construction costs. Authoritative estimates of *how much* range from 10 percent to 35 percent. This means that useless OSHA operations will add at least

$10 billion a year to what American consumers must pay for homes, apartments, highways, streets, subways, office buildings, and so on.

As one set of standards for this industry, OSHA adopted the safety provisions of the 1971 National Electric Code — making it applicable not only to buildings constructed after the code was adopted, but also to existing buildings. This means that OSHA *could require* the rewiring of practically every building in the United States constructed prior to 1971, even though the building complied with applicable local electric codes at the time it was constructed — and even though the codes it complied with may be more sensible and provide more safety than the code which OSHA imposes.

Similarly, other building-safety guidelines, blanketed into OSHA rules, *could require* all stairwells to be remodeled, all heating and ventilating systems to be revamped or replaced, in buildings throughout the United States and its territories.

In mid-1973, OSHA was preparing to impose on employers a new set of "workplace standards" devised and submitted in July 1972 by NIOSH. The standards involve exposure of workers to heat, noise, and "potential toxic substances." A real mare's-nest is here in the making. Medical science does not know and cannot find out how much is too much with regard to many of these factors. "Norms" are meaningless, because no human being is a norm. Each is an individual. What would make one man suffer might be pleasant to another.

Union officials (some of whom gleefully translate the OSHA acronym, "Our Savior Has Arrived") are angrily impatient for OSHA to adopt all of NIOSH's new workplace standards. The standards will provide an almost limitless number of contentious issues for unions to use as clubs to bludgeon management into concessions on matters that have nothing to do with the health and safety of employees. L.S. Beliczky, an official of United Rubber, Cork, Linoleum and Plastic Workers of America, is especially indignant about OSHA delay in fully implementing the new NIOSH standards. Mr. Beliczky says his union will not let management rest. If OSHA does not set the standards the union wants, the union will impose them in its next contract negotiations with management.

Mr. Beliczky is particularly interested in heat-stress. He tells about a heat-stress standard one of his locals has already imposed on plant management, indicating that this is the kind of standard he wants OSHA to force on all employers. It is a simple standard: "If the outdoor . . . temperature exceeds 90 degrees, all shifts will report for work and start work. But, if a senior union official thinks it is uncomfortable, management must conduct a vote of employees by secret ballot on whether or not the plant should shut down." Under "show-up" rules which unions usually impose, management must pay a full day's wages to any employee who shows up on a job but does not work because of weather.

The heat-stress standards which NIOSH has proposed are not quite as punitive against business as some union bosses want, but they are punitive. If adopted in their present form and fully enforced, they could close down for several months out of the year, or in every area of the nation where summers are long and hot, all construction, farm-and-ranch operations, and all other activity involving out-of-doors work by hired employees.

Management generally does everything feasible to make employees comfortable in uncomfortable working environments and to protect their health. Management provides respirators for employees exposed to harmful dust, ear plugs for those exposed to loud noise, fans to blow cool air on certain employees in unavoidably hot places. By such means, most businesses are already in compliance with some of the new NIOSH standards. But the OSHA statute has created a situation which threatens chaotic personnel difficulties and incalculable costs for management. An obscure provision of the law says that an employee may not be forced to wear a respirator if a doctor says he cannot "function normally" while wearing such a device. In that case, the employee "shall be rotated to another job or given the opportunity to transfer to a different position whose duties he is able to perform." The same provision could be enforced with regard to workers who cannot "function normally" while wearing ear plugs, or to those who cannot "function normally" in a hot place with cold air blowing on them. It is even conceivable that some employees could get a medical certification to keep them from wearing hard hats, clumsy safety shoes, goggles, or gloves that are hot and heavy. Under the OSHA statute, employees with long seniority could get transfers to easier, more comfortable work normally paying less than their old jobs, because it is more comfortable and requires less experience. They would replace lower-paid employees in the easier jobs, but they would have to be paid the same high wages as before.

An employer cited for an OSHA violation has 15 working days to give "notice of intent" to contest the citation. If he does not meet this deadline, the citation and the assessment of penalty "shall be deemed a final order . . . and not subject to review by any court or agency." If the employer files notice within the time limit, he may formally appeal for a hearing by the Occupational Safety and Health Review Commission, which was created by the OSHA statute as an administrative appellate court. The Review Commission sometimes displays hostility toward an employer who questions the fairness of OSHA citations.

McNeill Stokes, general counsel for the American Subcontractors Association, has had considerable experience with OSHA cases against employers. On September 14, 1972, Mr. Stokes testified before a House Select Subcommittee, saying:

There is a chilling effect on the employer's right to contest, because the OSHA Review Commission has taken the position that it can increase an employer's penalty if he chooses to contest. An election to appeal to a court may be a substantial risk for the employer in that a $1,000 per day penalty may accrue for each day that he is appealing . . . .

One of the cases which our firm is handling involves Beall Construction Company of Lincoln, Nebraska. The company received a $244 penalty for an alleged violation.

John Beall did not contest the fine because he felt that it was not economically practical for him to hire a lawyer to appeal the citation and proposed penalty through expensive and burdensome appeals.

Because he did not contest the citation, the basic fine and abatement order set by the inspector in the field became a final adjudication and was not subject to further review by any agency or court.

John Beall then wrote a letter to Senator Carl T. Curtis (Nebraska) supporting his proposed amendments to the Occupational Safety and Health Act.

Several months later the area director of the Occupational Safety and Health Administration in Omaha, Nebraska, spoke to Hugh Beall (also of Beall Construction Company, and John Beall's brother) on the telephone accusing him of writing a letter criticizing the act to Senator Curtis.

Approximately three days later, federal inspectors reinspected the worksite and alleged that Beall had not abated the safety violations.

Beall was fined $750 per day for each day that the safety violation had not been corrected, which amounted to $31,744, which is a high price to pay for exercising a citizen's constitutional right to communicate with his elected representatives.

Beall must now take the offense to prove himself innocent and contest the daily penalties. As a small businessman, he finds it economically depressing since the fine is more than double his annual income.

McNeill Stokes also told about the case against Fred Horne's Plumbing and Heating Company, which employs ten persons and has an excellent safety program and record. On a construction job in Atlanta, some of Mr. Horne's employees (without his knowledge, in disobedience to his specific instructions, in defiance of the warnings of other employees working nearby, and in contradiction of established practice which they had themselves observed on previous similar jobs) refused to construct wood shoring to protect themselves against cave-ins in a ditch where they were working. The ditch embankment caved in, killing one of the employees. As a result, OSHA fined Horne $600 for failure to have proper shoring in place. Horne appealed the fine. As attorney who handled this case for Mr. Horne, McNeill Stokes says:

"When we contested the citation and . . . penalty, the [OSHA] inspectors issued an additional $1800 in penalties against the employer because this employer had the gall to contest the citation and proposed penalties for an offense of which he was innocent."

Occasionally the "supreme court" of the judicial branch of OSHA (that is, the Review

Commission) will rebuke a "lower court" of OSHA for trying to show a little leniency toward business. A compliance officer found a company in "serious violation" of an OSHA safety rule. Reviewing the case, an administrative-law judge classified the violation as "other than serious," because the employer had a good safety record, because only one worker was ever exposed to the cited hazard, and because it was improbable that he would ever suffer a serious injury because of the hazard. In May 1973, the Review Commission reversed the judge, holding that limited exposure and improbability of serious injury were no defense, and ruling that an infraction of an OSHA safety rule must be judged according to the severity of *any* injury that *might* result.

The stated statutory purpose of OSHA is to ease the economic burden imposed on commerce by work-caused injuries and illnesses. But OSHA will never achieve any significant reduction in work-caused injuries and illnesses unless it closes down a significant portion of American industry; and the economic burdens OSHA itself imposes on commerce are greater than those it is supposed to ease.

Yet, the Congress certainly was aware of the load it was putting on American employers when it passed OSHA. One section of the Act says: "Any information obtained . . . under this Act shall be obtained with a minimum burden upon employers, especially those operating small businesses." Another section authorizes Small

60

Business Administration loans to employers "likely to suffer substantial economic injury" from making costly changes to comply with OSHA orders.

James D. McClary, president of the Associated General Contractors (a trade association representing major firms in the building industry), admits that OSHA rules and enforcement procedures are burdensome, if not vicious, but says: "We can't buck the objectives of the safety law. We're for one." He means that most big builders are *afraid* — afraid of incurring the wrath and invoking the vengeance of powerful federal and union officials; afraid of the OSHA-crats themselves; afraid of getting a bad public image for opposing the "objectives" of a law which has been fraudulently sold as a means of providing safety for workers.

This attitude of going along to get along seems to characterize most of the trade associations representing employers. Employers find themselves trapped, confused, or scared by OSHA. They turn to their trade association for help. By way of "serving" its members, the association tells them they must learn to live with OSHA, offers them (for a special price, usually) digests of applicable OSHA regulations, and promises to keep them informed of any new regulations. The association may lobby with Members of Congress to get the statute reformed a bit, but OSHA's harassments make the association more important to its business members — the association executives like that, and will go along for their own advantage.

Businessmen must, of course, do their best to comply with OSHA as long as it is in force, but they should never compromise with it. And they must recognize that OSHA cannot be reformed into something tolerable. Even if it were not harming business, it would not be acceptable, because it is not constitutional. Congress created OSHA and feeds it with our tax money, to prowl the land and prey on us. Congress should be forced to abolish it.

Chapter Six

The FDA
Con Game

THE Food and Drug Administration is a relatively minor regulatory agency, but it exercises major influence in many large industries. In general, its activities (especially in recent years) reflect its anti-business origins.

Government regulation of food and drugs began with the Pure Food and Drug Act of 1906, establishing federal controls over the *manufacture* of food and drugs, *in federal territories and districts only*. The bill was not intended to give government control over the food and drug industries, but to prohibit the production and distribution of adulterated or misbranded foods and drugs in, and from, areas over which the federal government has constitutional jurisdiction. This law went as far as the federal government can constitutionally go "to regulate commerce" in food and drugs.

In 1938, however, the New Deal Congress enacted the federal Food, Drug, and Cosmetic Act, creating the Food and Drug Administration (FDA) to establish and enforce standards of identity and quality for food, drugs, and cosmetics produced anywhere in the United States. During the next two decades there were sporadic, but unsuccessful, efforts to tighten government controls. A determined drive began in the late 1950's.

In September 1959, John Lear, science editor of the "Liberal" *Saturday Review of Literature*, demanded a Congressional investigation of drug marketing, alleging that "rich and powerful corporations" were exploiting "the results of new scientific research discoveries." Lear recommended the publication *Medical Letter* as a competent authority in the field of drug marketing. The managing director of *Medical Letter* was Arthur Kallett, an identified Communist.

In December 1959, the Senate Judiciary Antitrust and Monopoly Subcommittee (under the chairmanship of Estes Kefauver) began holding televised hearings investigating the drug industry.

Kefauver's star witness against the industry was Dr. Louis Lasagna, who was on the advisory board of *Medical Letter*. Lasagna had formerly been a special medical advisor for Consumers Union, which Arthur Kallett had founded in the 1920's and which had been cited years before the hearings as a Communist front. Dr. John M. Blair was chief economist of the Kefauver Subcommittee staff. Dr. Blair was the author of a book (*Seeds of Destruction*, 1938) asserting that private capitalism is doomed because it contains fundamental weaknesses which are the seeds of its own destruction. Dr. J.D. Glover of Harvard University accused Dr. Blair of "pettifoggery and efforts, not to analyze the facts, but to handle the data in such a way as to 'make a case' against big business.'' Senator John Marshall Butler (R.-Md.), after reviewing all hearings and reports by the Kefauver Subcommittee, said he could not find "one iota of evidence" that the Subcommittee had "made any serious attempt" to do anything except air the economic theories of Dr. Blair.

In fact, neither in the Kefauver Subcommittee hearings nor in all the other propaganda for new controls on the drug industry was proof ever presented of a single instance of harm to the health of the American people resulting from the absence of the kind of controls being proposed. Little effort was made to show that a new law was necessary to protect the public from harmful drugs. The case for tighter controls rested on the claim that the public needed protection from high prices being charged by the "monopolistic" drug industry.

The new bill was called the Drug Industry Act. Senator Kefauver introduced it on April 12, 1961; President Kennedy gave it his blessing on April 10, 1962; and the Senate Judiciary Committee reported it favorably in mid-July of 1962. This bit of legislative history is outlined to show how brilliant the timing of expert manipulators of public opinion can sometimes be. The Judiciary Committee's favorable report on the Drug Industry Act was made at a time when the nation's news media were featuring stories about Thalidomide, a German-made tranquilizing drug which was found to have caused malformation of babies in Europe. The case of a pregnant Arizona woman who had taken Thalidomide purchased in London by her husband dominated national news for several days. On August 1, 1962, President Kennedy announced that, because of the "Thalidomide disaster," he was recommending a 25 percent increase in FDA appropriations. He urged quick action on the pending Drug Industry Act, saying: "It is clear that to prevent even more serious disasters from occurring in this country in the future, additional legislative safeguards are necessary."

Surrounded by "disasters," fore and aft and on the flanks, all of which they could be shielded against by the proposed legislation, the people presumably were expected to forget that the new law had not been designed to protect them against disasters. It had been "intended" to protect their pocketbooks. For a pregnant woman to discover that she is bearing a malformed baby is, unquestionably, a tragedy for her and her husband; but for the President of the United States to call it a national disaster is a bit extreme. Moreover, since the drug which caused the sad affair was made in Germany and sold in England, it is difficult to see how a law controlling the American drug industry could do much about the situation. Nonetheless, the public seems to have been bamboozled by the rigged sensationalism. At least, public opposition to the new control law was quickly swept aside.

Opponents of the Drug Industry Act pointed out that medical and pharmaceutical professionals are better qualified than government agencies to determine the safety of drugs. The free force of competition is more effective than government regulation in protecting the public against both harm and high prices. When government takes control of the drug industry, prices are more likely to go up than down. Quality and progress will decline. When a federal agency can make or break a company by giving or withholding its blessing, drug companies are likely to de-emphasize the research and development required to outpace competitors; they will tend to concentrate their primary effort on currying favor with the all-powerful regulators. This will create in the drug industry, as it has already done in other heavily regulated industries, a potential breeding ground for waste, stupidity, graft, and corruption. The law will not decrease market domination by giants in the industry and thus open more opportunity for small businesses, as the law's sponsors promise; it will do the opposite. In a tightly regulated industry (airlines, for example), the market is generally dominated by a few major firms who are favorites of the regulators. None will struggle mightily to provide better products and prices than others, because all alike will be operating under standards set by the FDA.

Opponents of the new Drug Industry Act also cited the record. Even under the unconstitutional controls of the Food, Drug, and Cosmetic Act of 1938, the American drug industry had been the freest on earth, and because of that freedom it had produced more new, beneficial drugs than had been produced in all other countries combined. Approximately two-thirds of all new drugs being prescribed by British doctors were developed by American drug firms, whereas, prior to socialized medicine and rigid government control of drug production in Great Britain, the British had made outstanding contributions in the general fields of biochemistry and physiology, and in the particular field of developing "miracle drugs." In the Soviet Union, the drug industry (totally controlled by the Communist government) had not produced one new drug product of consequence in the 45 years since the Communists took control. This historical record should be considered seriously, since Communists and other socialists are behind the drug-industry-control law being proposed for the United States.

All these arguments by opponents of the new control law were ignored. The Senate, by unanimous roll-call vote, passed the Drug Industry Act of 1962 on August 23. The House passed it on September 27. A Conference Bill was quickly approved by both chambers, and President Kennedy signed it into law on October 10.

Recent statistics indicate that opponents of the Drug Industry Act of 1962 made some correct predictions. In 1962, FDA approved marketing of 155 new drugs, out of 626 applications made by the drug industry. In 1972, FDA approved 26 applications out of 229.

Since enactment of the Drug Industry Act of 1962, FDA activities have ranged far beyond the simple purpose of protecting the health, or even the pocketbooks, of the public. Some FDA regulations reflect the snobbery of all regulators and arrangers of other peoples' lives: they try to keep people from making purchases which FDA officials regard as unnecessary or in bad taste. Some FDA regulations are vengeful.

For a long time, FDA officials have been trying to regulate the health-food industry out of existence – with labeling requirements that are costly; that compel the makers of vitamins and food supplements to discredit their own products; that require them to pay tribute to their principal competitor, the regular-food industry.

The FDA has never alleged that vitamins and food supplements are harmful to health, but merely that they are unnecessary and that the public spends too much money on them. The FDA wants to protect the people against spending their money in ways which the FDA considers wasteful. This is why FDA has tried to impose labeling regulations which would require health-food packagers to discredit their own products. As FDA Commissioner James Lee Goddard explained in 1966: "We can only hope to educate people on this vitamin problem. We won't order vitamin pills off the market."

The FDA's hostile attitude toward the health food industry was more recently expressed (1973) by Dr. Ogden C. Johnson, head of the nutrition division of FDA. Asked to comment on "organic foods" or "natural foods," Dr. Johnson said:

> I keep praying at night that the market will just disappear. It should not have to be legalized out, but people should be aware of the deceptions. For instance, there is much more organic produce SOLD than is GROWN. Take "turbinado" sugar, which is unrefined, so dirty the industry considers it unfit to use. Yet it is sold in health-food stores for as much as $1.95 per pound . . . . Regular sugar is seven cents per pound.
>
> What is a "natural" food? Does anything you do that reduces nutrients then make it non-natural? . . . Does peeling an orange make it less natural?

With a rather vigorous lobby of its own, the health-food industry long resisted the worst proposals made by FDA. In 1973, however, FDA issued a new set of proposed labeling regulations which, if they stand, could destroy the health-food industry. The new regulations resulted, in part, from lobbying for new labeling regulations *by the chief spokesman for the health-food industry.*

The chief spokesman for the health-food industry is the National Health Federation (NHF), organized in 1955. It calls itself a "noncommercial health consumer group." Unlike practically every other organization that calls itself a "consumer group," NHF is run by people who seem to be conservatively oriented. Unfortunately, however, they are not Constitutional conservatives. And thereby hangs an interesting tale.

The NHF and Constitutional conservatives have worked together on important issues — such as opposing the fluoridation of public water supplies — but they have not always stood on the same grounds.

Most Constitutional conservatives think fluoridated water is a hazard to health; but even if they thought it beneficial, they would still oppose government fluoridation of public water supplies. Why? A nation which values anything — even good health — more than it values freedom will lose its freedom. Government has no valid authority to force all the people to use water medicated with fluorides, solely because some people think a fraction of the population might benefit from such coercion. Governmental power should be limited, not by what government officials or even a majority of the people consider good or bad at any given time, but by a binding constitution which only the people can change by the deliberate process prescribed by that Constitution. That is the Constitutional conservatives' rationale in opposing fluoridation of public water supplies.

The NHF stand on fluoridation is pragmatic. The NHF opposes fluoridation because the NHF thinks it harmful to health. Which means that the NHF would approve fluoridating public water supplies if the NHF thought it would be beneficial to the health of the public. This assumption about what the National Health

Federation *would do* can be safely deduced from what it *did do* with regard to food labeling. What the NHF did do demonstrates that good people can sometimes get into bad trouble if they engage in lobbying or other political activities without using fundamental principles as a guide.

Early in 1971, five militant activists (law students at George Washington University) began a legal attack on that part of the "Establishment" represented by the regular-food industry. Using the name LABEL, Inc., the five students petitioned the FDA to promulgate a regulation requiring food processors and packagers to use labels including a complete listing of all the ingredients in processed or fabricated foods. The FDA rejected the petition, saying it lacked authority to require such labeling.

Thereupon, the National Health Federation joined forces with LABEL and filed a lawsuit to force FDA to impose upon the NHF's old enemy, the regular-food industry, the labeling requirements that the NHF wanted. The NHF said its aim was to protect consumers by forcing the food industry to let consumers know exactly what they are buying. But the NHF and LABEL lost the lawsuit. On January 31, 1973, the U.S. Court of Appeals in the District of Columbia held that the FDA does not, in fact, have legal authority to require the kind of labeling that the NHF and LABEL want. But the matter did not end there.

While the NHF and LABEL case to force

FDA to promulgate new food-labeling regulations was moving through the courts, the FDA was fabricating new food-labeling regulations.

On January 19, 1973, the FDA issued a massive set of proposed food-labeling regulations. Dr. Charles C. Edwards, FDA commissioner, announced that the new regulations "mark the beginning of the new era in providing consumers with complete, concise, and informative food labeling."

The FDA still contends, however, that it has no authority to *require* such labeling. At present, the regulations are mere recommendations, but FDA hopes they will soon "become law." Explaining, FDA's Dr. Ogden C. Johnson said: "Food labeling is still voluntary, but probably within the next two legislative sessions it will become law."

At a two-day food-labeling seminar in Denver during May of 1973, Dr. Johnson explained and defended the new regulations. They will require, he pointed out, that labels list ingredients in order of their predominance in the product; then list the nutritive values in a single serving, including calories, grams of protein, fat, and carbohydrate; then list important proteins, vitamins, and minerals according to percentages of RDA (Recommended Daily Allowances). Dr. Johnson said:

"The label will be like a small textbook, but people will have to know more about nutrition to understand the label. The RDA material is based on the metric system. We had better get used to the metric system, and nutrition is a good place to start. We have five people in FDA now interpreting our work."

Asked about the cost of the proposed labeling, Dr. Johnson said: "It depends on the size of the company and the size of the market. Some firms spend money unnecessarily."

Dr. Dee M. Graham, head of the department of food science and nutrition at the University of Missouri, also participated in the food-labeling seminar. Dr. Graham declared: "The FDA detailed recipe-type regulations have been hailed as a major triumph by many consumerists. I feel they are a disaster for the consumer . . . . Food labeling as proposed by FDA portends major cost increases for processor and consumer . . . . FDA's proposals are fraught with administrative chaos, and create wide new staging areas from which militant consumer activists can launch even more damaging attacks on the FDA, the food industry, and our entire food system . . . . I find the FDA food labeling proposals appalling."

National Health Federation officials were at first jubilant about the new FDA food-labeling proposals; but after wading through the hundreds of pages of regulations, they too were appalled — but not because the labels will be complicated textbooks-in-miniature which can be understood only by nutrition experts who are familiar with the metric system of weights and measures; and not because they are being imposed by a bureaucracy which obviously has no conception of, or concern about, the additional cost they will add to everyone's grocery bill. Rather, NHF officials were *annoyed* because the labeling regulations were not made mandatory upon the regular-food industry *at once*. They were *appalled* because they found in the new FDA rules a big section dealing with health foods. In a regulation applying only to foods for special dietary use (health foods) the FDA prohibits packagers, processors, and distributors from:

● Claiming, or suggesting, that products intended to supplement diets are sufficient in themselves to prevent, treat, or cure disease;

● Implying that a diet of ordinary foods cannot supply adequate nutrients;

● Claiming that inadequacy or insufficiency of nutrients in the diet is due to the soil in which foods are grown;

● Claiming that transportation, storage, or cooking of foods can result in inadequate or deficient nutrients in the diet;

● Implying that a natural vitamin in a food is superior to an added or synthetic vitamin, or that there is a difference between vitamins naturally present in foods and those that have been added.

If the health-food industry can make none of these claims, it will have no means of persuading people to buy health foods. The industry will die; and consumers who are already convinced that health foods are beneficial to their health will no longer have the freedom to buy them because government will have regulated them out of existence.

Concerning these harsh prohibitions which the FDA will impose on the health-food industry, the NHF correctly asserts: "Unless Congress, through legislative enactment, prohibits this action, a manufacturer or distributor of [food] supplements could be imprisoned for making literally true and scientifically accurate statements, in context, in labeling foods and/or food supplements even though the products are not adulterated, deleterious or toxic."

Thus the National Health Federation, which had been lobbying and taking legal action to force FDA to require certain food labeling, reversed course and started lobbying activities and legal action to prevent FDA from requiring certain food labeling.

And the NHF announced its support of the Hosmer Bill, H.R. 643. This bill specifies: (1) that truthful nutritional claims for foods and food supplements may be made on labels and in advertising; and (2) that foods and food supplements are not drugs and cannot be regulated as such by the FDA.

The NHF also announced that it was taking legal action in federal court — asking the court "to rule on the legality of the implementation by bureaus of regulations having the effect of law, by simply publishing their rules and regulations in the *Federal Register* without the approval of Congress." That is striking at the heart of the tyrannical, unconstitutional, "administrative law" system which Congress has spawned and nourished in the United States; and it needs to be done. The NHF officials seem to be quite unaware, however, that, in their court case against the FDA, they are expressing outrage about the FDA's doing to them precisely what they previously had tried to force the FDA to do to others.

If American business is ever to remove the burden of excessive government regulation from its shoulders, businessmen must stop trying to use government to bludgeon their competition and unite behind constitutional principles in the interests of a free economy which best serves us all.

Chapter Seven

Farming And Framing The Taxpayers

FARMING, like manufacturing, is a business. And it may surprise you to learn that the federal farm laws, like all other federal laws to regulate business activities, are descendants of the Interstate Commerce Act of 1887 and of the Sherman Antitrust Act of 1890.

In 1929, the price of wheat was falling, while general living costs were rising. Congress enacted, and President Herbert Hoover signed, the Farm Stabilization Act, authorizing the federal government to buy wheat in order to bolster the market. The government bought and stored 257 million bushels of wheat. That did bolster the price of wheat for a while; but in 1931 and 1932 the government dumped the stored wheat on the market, driving the price of wheat down to the lowest level in history. Many small family farmers, who were pinched in 1929 before government "helped" them, were bankrupt because of that help by the end of 1932.

That was the beginning of federal farm programs.

In 1933, Communists in President Franklin D. Roosevelt's Department of Agriculture conceived a farm program which Congress authorized with the Agricultural Adjustment Act (AAA) of 1933. In 1936, the Supreme Court (in the Butler Case) held the AAA of 1933 to be unconstitutional. It *was* unconstitutional, and so was the Farm Stabilization Act of 1929. The Constitution gives the federal government no power to regulate or subsidize farming; and the Tenth Amendment says that powers not delegated to the federal government are reserved to states or to the people. Nonetheless, in 1938 Congress enacted another Agricultural Adjustment Act, authorizing even more illegal intervention in the farming business than the 1933 law had authorized. By 1938, President Roosevelt had seated a New Deal majority on the Supreme Court; and the Court approved the AAA of 1938. All subsequent federal farm laws have been amendments of, or additions to, that 1938 Act.

The publicly stated purpose of the Communist-conceived farm programs of the 1930's was to save the small family farmers, the backbone of the nation, who were foundering in the Great Depression. To that end, farmers were paid to destroy crops and animals instead of selling them at low prices to a public that was paying high prices for foreign imports of the same kinds of foodstuffs that American farmers were destroying. The government also bought farm commodities and held them in storage to keep them from being sold to American consumers at low prices — even as consumers were paying high prices for foreign imports of the same commodities.

Thus bluntly outlined, the farm program seems unbelievable, even nightmarish. But government contrived to justify and explain it with a word: *surplus*. The farmer was suffering because he could not get good prices for what he produced; prices were low because he was producing "too much"; therefore, the farmer would be uplifted and the entire national economy along with him if government eliminated the *surplus*, either by destroying surplus farm commodities, by storing them to keep them off the market, or by inducing farmers not to produce "too much." That was the rationale.

The fact is that American farmers never did produce too much. Because of economic distortion caused by government during and following World War I, our national economy had made wild swings upward and downward, and eventually plunged into the Great Depression of the 1930's. Farmers and other producers were getting low prices not because production was too great, but because public buying power was too small. Such economic explanations of why the farmer was in bad shape would not have won public acceptance of the government's strange farm program because too few Americans had any understanding of basic economics, but the *surplus* rationale did; and *surplus* became the buzz word in all federal farm programs.

President Truman proposed replacing the complicated Roosevelt farm programs with the Brannan Plan, which had the virtue of elemental simplicity: it would have authorized direct federal payments to give farmers the minimum annual income that officialdom wanted them to have, regardless of merit, production, market demands, or anything else. Congress rejected the Brannan Plan, and the Roosevelt farm programs continued.

Although President Truman never got a farm program of his own, he did initiate (1949) the first International Wheat Agreement, by which a number of wheat-producing nations agreed to regulate production, price, and distribution of wheat throughout the world. This replacing of the free market with an international government cartel did keep the price of wheat high for consumers, but it did not help American farmers. Our government enforced the terms of the treaty on Americans; other nations enforced or ignored the treaty as they pleased, giving their farmers an advantage over ours in competing for world markets. (The International Wheat Agreement was extended several times, eventually being replaced, in 1968, by the International Grains Arrangement, which established a broader, tighter cartel than the wheat agreement had created.)

By the time Dwight Eisenhower became President (1953), federal farm programs had already cost consumers many billions of dollars in federal taxes alone, not to mention the immeasurable costs of government-enforced higher prices. The government had some $5 billion dollars' worth of surplus farm commodities in storage; and the storage costs were averaging about half a million dollars a day.

In 1954, President Eisenhower started a new

program to solve the farm surplus problem. He initiated "Food For Freedom" (later called "Food For Peace," the change, perhaps, reflecting the growth of the better-Red-than-dead attitude that freedom is less important than peace). The Food For Peace program was authorized by the Agricultural Trade Development and Assistance Act of 1954. Under this law (still operating), we sell or give our farm products to foreign nations, some of the biggest recipients being Communist nations. The sales are paid for in the local currency of the recipients. Then we use some of the currency to pay expenses of our missions in the country, but most goes back as foreign aid.

In a separate effort to solve the farm surplus problem, President Eisenhower also initiated, in 1954, compulsory wheat acreage allotments. Prior to that, participation in the government's wheat control program had been voluntary. If a wheat farmer chose not to participate, he could plant as much wheat as he was able, but received no federal subsidy for any of it. Almost without exception, managers of large corporate farming operations and tax-exempt farmers' cooperatives accepted those earlier government controls in order to get subsidies, but not the men on small family-size farms, who constituted a big majority of all wheat farmers. Most small wheat farmers chose not to participate in the government's voluntary wheat control programs, rejecting government handouts for themselves, even though they were being taxed to pay for handouts to their competitors.

The compulsory program which Eisenhower started in 1954, however, forced acreage controls on all wheat farmers, whether they accepted federal subsidies or not. Then began what many wheat farmers called "the Reign of Terror by the Wheat Police." Is that a propaganda phrase which grossly exaggerates the actual situation? Not entirely. The Wheat Police were Department of Agriculture personnel who administered and enforced the compulsory wheat acreage allotments.

These federal agents trespassed upon a farmer's property, without warrants or other legal authorization, to see whether he was growing wheat. If they found that he was, they tramped around measuring his fields to determine whether he was growing too much. If the farmer objected to such illegal trespass, a federal court would issue, not a valid search warrant, but an order restraining him from interfering with federal agents. If the farmer still resisted the illegal trespass, he would be jailed without trial for contempt of court. If the Wheat Police decided that the farmer was growing too much wheat, they ordered him to sign a questionnaire admitting his guilt. If he refused, a federal court would order him to do it. If he still refused, he would be jailed without trial. The Wheat Police who illegally searched a farm assumed a judicial role to assess penalties against the farmer. If the farmer did not pay, the Wheat Police would seize his bank account, his personal property, or his farm — or all of them. If he resisted, he would be jailed without trial.

These are not conjectures about what theoretically could have happened. It actually did happen, time and again, in a great many cases. In the single year of 1955, the first year after compulsory wheat acreage allotment began, the federal government fined 14,000 American farmers a total of more than $8.5 million. Not one of them was charged with fraud, embezzlement, theft, or other crime. Not one was charged with illegally getting price-support payments from the government. All were fined solely for growing "too much" wheat on their own farms. Most of them were small farmers, who raised wheat as feed for their own livestock, asking no subsidies or other favors from government.

In a program employing thousands of federal agents regulating millions of farmers and dispensing hundreds of millions of tax dollars to them as price supports, there were bound to be many cases of bribery and other criminal acts involving misuse of public funds; but the government seemed indifferent about this. Such common criminal acts were no threat to government's assumed power to control the business of farming; but farmer resistance to the controls did present such a threat. If one farmer, by legal process, could successfully resist government regulation, he would jeopardize the whole structure of government controls over private economic activities. As in Communist countries, violators of the economic commands of government were considered more dangerous than criminals. Hence, they were summarily punished without due process of law.

The attitude of most federal courts in Wheat Police cases was like that of the Supreme Court in the Ohio fire-marshal case recounted by Lowell Mason. In this case the court sanctioned the jailing of a man without due process because he was accused, not of crime, but of behavior "damaging to the economy." Note the expressed attitude of U.S. District Judge Frank L. Kloeb at Toledo, Ohio, in 1956. Irritated because so many wheat farmers were coming into his court trying to test the constitutionality of the Agricultural Adjustment Act, Judge Kloeb called such efforts "preposterous." He said that he would refuse "absolutely to go into the question of constitutionality" of the Act, and that he was going to start "handing out stiff sentences" to farmers trying to raise the question.

One U.S. District Judge (T. Whitfield Davidson in Dallas, presiding in a Wheat Police case against J. Evetts Haley Jr.) did declare the Agricultural Adjustment Act unconstitutional. He was tersely overruled by the Supreme Court, which refused to hear arguments from Haley's attorneys, or even to explain its decision.

On August 28, 1957, President Eisenhower approved a law which had been urged by his concerned Agriculture Secretary, Ezra Taft Benson, allowing small farmers to grow up to thirty acres of wheat for their own use. That did not restore freedom to farming, of course, but it did bring to an end the brief era called the Reign of

Terror by the Wheat Police. The Reign began in 1954 to help eliminate farm surpluses; when it ended in 1957, the government had more than nine billion dollars' worth of farm commodities in storage — almost twice as much as in 1954.

In 1956, the government initiated another new program to solve the farm surplus problem. Twenty-three years before, as was pointed out earlier, Democrats had attacked this problem by paying farmers to destroy crops and animals already raised. Then, the Democrats had drifted into the price-support program — in effect, paying farmers not to grow certain crops on a portion of their land, but allowing unsubsidized crops to be grown on that portion. Now, the Eisenhower Republicans started the Soil Bank — paying owners to keep their land idle and not raise any crops at all.

Legalized racketeering in the government's farm programs multiplied rapidly under the Soil Bank law. There were literally thousands of cases comparable to that of the Wayne E. Tallman Farms Company of Kiowa County, Colorado. Wayne Tallman bought a 6,960-acre ranch for $139,200, and then, through a maze of complicated subleasing arrangements, put 3,879 acres of the ranch in the Soil Bank in such a way that the government, over a ten-year period, paid him $271,000 for not growing any crops on those 3,879 acres of ranch land. During that time, however, he was free to pasture the 3,879 acres, and to use the remaining 3,081 acres of his ranch as he pleased. All of this was legal under the Soil Bank law. In fact, Tallman took the precaution of getting prior official approval of the deal from the Agricultural Stabilization Committee of Kiowa County. In essence, the government had *given* Tallman his 6,960-acre ranch, plus a net cash bonus of $131,800 for not growing crops during a ten-year period on part of the ranch he was given.

The Soil Bank program lasted ten years. The 1956 law that created it authorized about $750 million a year in direct cash payments to landowners *for taking productive land out of cultivation.* Just before passing that law, Congress enacted, and President Eisenhower signed, another law authorizing a dam and irrigation project on the upper Colorado River, for the purpose of *irrigating and putting into cultivation* a vast acreage of high, arid land never before cultivated. To farm economists, none of this made sense.

In 1963, President Kennedy proposed to solve the farm problem with the Cochrane Plan, which prescribed a "supply-management" system closely resembling collective farming in Communist countries. Congress rejected the Cochrane Plan but enacted President Kennedy's Feed Grains Program — supporting prices without requiring any curtailment of production.

During President Johnson's Administration, Congress enacted the Food and Agriculture Act of 1965. It was technically different in several ways from previous and subsequent farm laws. In essence, however, the program it authorized is still operating. *How* it is operating is revealed by a statistical report published in the *Congressional Record,* March 26, 1970 (Pages E2536-E2579), the latest detailed study that has been made public.

In the 1970 fiscal year, according to that report, a total of $555 million was given to landowners for not growing certain crops on portions of their acreage, and for price supports on crops which they did grow. Most of this money, which of course came from taxes, went to wealthy landowners, some of whom were banks, huge conglomerates, and foreign corporations. In the 1969 calendar year, 79 big farming companies in eight states got more than $200,000 *each* for not growing certain crops on certain parts of their acreage. The largest individual recipients were in Kings County, California, where three agri-business firms got more than $7.8 million: the J.G. Boswell Company, $4.4 million; South Lake Farms, $1.8 million; the Salyer Land Company, $1.6 million. The Delta and Pine Land Company in Mississippi (a British-owned corporation) got $731,772. And Wayne Tallman of Kiowa County, Colorado, who had done so well under the Soil Bank program of 1956, was still farming the taxpayers in 1969. In that year, for not growing specified crops on certain portions of his available acreage, Mr. Tallman received $47,002 from the federal government; and the Wayne E. Tallman Farms Company of the same county got $39,410.

President Johnson never did propose, and

President Nixon has not yet proposed, anything new in the way of a farm program, although Mr. Nixon has talked volubly about "unshackling our farmers." During the Johnson and Nixon years, however, other government programs have had great impact on farming — especially programs in the operations of the Poverty War and of foreign policy.

On the West Coast, government Poverty-War lawyers openly support Cesar Chavez, a leftist revolutionary who is trying to force farm workers to join his Communist-dominated United Farm Workers Organizing Committee (UFWOC, or UFWO). Chavez wants to acquire monopolistic control over all farm labor in the country; with such power, he could put an end to free-enterprise farming by forcing collectivized agriculture on the nation. Poverty-War personnel on the federal payroll helped Chavez organize UFWO; they have used tax money in his behalf; they have helped organize, finance, and lead picketing and demonstrations (some of them violent) in support of Chavez and UFWO; they have used their influence with the news media and with leftist political, social, and religious leaders to arrange national boycotts of grapes, lettuce, and so on. These boycotts are not intended to get anything for farm workers. They are used as economic pressure to require farmers to force their own employees into Chavez's union.

The most visible damage done to American farmers by Johnson-Nixon policies, however, has resulted from foreign policy operations.

On February 10, 1966 (less than nine years after President Eisenhower's Wheat Police were riding roughshod over American farmers for producing too much wheat), President Johnson told Congress that American farmers must be induced to produce more wheat and other foodstuffs. This would be necessary for implementation of a plan which Mr. Johnson asked Congress to authorize − a plan by which American taxpayers would feed the world.

President Johnson harked back to the previous 12 years, during which, in the Food For Peace program, the United States had given away millions of tons of "surplus" food, worth some $25 billion, to help feed people abroad. Johnson expressed pride in that activity, but acknowledged that "the problem of world hunger is more serious today than ever before." It appears that the more we feed the people abroad, the faster they multiply and the less they produce for themselves. Evidently, however, President Johnson figured that Americans can produce and give away food faster than the rest of the world can breed. He asked Congress to provide incentives (tax money) for greater agricultural production, saying that we must move beyond the concept of merely giving foreigners our surplus production: we must produce food especially for them.

Johnson made his feed-the-world proposal at a time when American food supplies for home consumption were running low. On July 1, 1966, the Department of Agriculture estimated

90

that American wheat stocks were about 536 million bushels — 64 million bushels below what the Department considered a safe minimum stock. Combined U.S. holdings of corn, oats, grain sorghums, and barley were 24 percent below average. At that time, however, we were daily feeding, with our grain, 64 million people in 52 foreign countries.

On July 4, 1966, *U.S. News & World Report* commented: "A flood of wheat has been pouring from U.S. bins to ease hunger abroad . . . . While others [Australia and Canada] are selling their wheat for hard cash, the United States, badly in need of foreign earnings, is giving away or selling for soft currency much of its wheat. India alone is getting almost as much U.S. wheat this year as Americans themselves will consume."

Congress did not authorize President Johnson's world-feeding scheme in 1966, but it did extend the twelve-year-old Food For Peace program another two years — at a tax cost of $2.5 billion per year.

Poverty-War programs which aggravated the problems of farmers during the Johnson régime continue unabated under the Nixon Administration. That part of President Nixon's foreign policy which produced the 1972 wheat deal with the Soviet Union has had a sensational impact, not just on the farming business, but on the whole national economy. The deal had many ramifications.

The Soviets, in need of foodstuffs to allay

incipient revolt in their slave empire, where widespread famine was impending, wanted to buy American farm commodities on credit guaranteed by the U.S. Government. Historically, *credit* to the Soviets means *gift*. They still owe us the $628 million they owed us when President Roosevelt gave them diplomatic recognition in 1933. Our government has long since written off that old debt. It is seldom mentioned any more, and the public is unaware of it. But the public *is* aware that the Soviets owe us $11 billion for our Lend-Lease aid to them during World War II.

The last negotiations to settle the old World War II debt had been broken off in 1960. At that time, we offered to let the Soviets settle the $11 billion debt for $800 million — a little over 7 cents on the dollar. The best they offered was $300 million — about 2.6 cents on the dollar.

In 1971, the Soviets agreed to reopen negotiations on the old debt if the United States would grant them credits to buy American products and also grant them most-favored-nation tariff treatment (meaning drastic reduction of tariffs on what they sell here, so that their commodities — vodka, for example — can flow into the United States more freely). Negotiations were resumed.

The Soviets agreed to pay $722 million in settlement of the old $11 billion debt (about 6.6 cents on the dollar). Mr. Nixon agreed to sell them $750 million worth of grain over a three-year period — $500 million of the sale to be on credit (at 6.12 percent interest) guaranteed by the U.S. Government. President Nixon also agreed to give the Soviets the tariff reductions they want, if he can get Congressional approval. If Congress does not approve the tariff reduction, the President will compensate the Soviets by reducing from $722 million to $48 million the amount they are asked to pay in settlement of the old $11 billion debt.

This Nixon-Soviet agreement was completed on July 8, 1972. In the month just prior to that, domestic prices of American wheat had risen considerably. Before the rise, however, most farmers had already sold their wheat to grain dealers. By mid-September 1972, the Soviets had bought 400 million bushels of wheat, most of it from six giant grain dealers, who had close contacts inside the Department of Agriculture. The domestic price of wheat at the time the dealers sold to the Soviets was much higher than it had been when they bought the wheat from farmers.

The grain dealers and the Nixon Administration denied that there had been any collusion or advance leaks of information. Most wheat farmers felt abused, however. If the Department of Agriculture, which is supposed to look after farmers, had let them know that wheat prices would soon rise, they could have held their wheat for better prices.

Let it not be supposed that the Soviets paid dearly for American wheat because they bought at a time when domestic prices were high. Our government shielded the Soviets against that with our tax money. Because of government price supports, the American domestic price of wheat is nearly always higher than world prices. Therefore, the government subsidizes exports of wheat. American grain dealers sell wheat to foreign purchasers at world prices; the government gives the dealers the difference between world prices and domestic prices. On the wheat the Soviets bought, our government paid export subsidies totaling about $300 million. The giant grain dealers got the money; Communists got the wheat and the savings; American taxpayers got to pay the bill.

That was just the beginning of the cost to American taxpayer-consumers. The wheat sale to the Soviets was a major factor in sending food prices soaring in the United States. The price of bread and other foods made from wheat went up dramatically. Prices of cattle feed (in short supply because of the sale to the Soviets) rose sharply, and so, consequently, did the price of beef. Shock waves traveled throughout the economy. Railroads pressed into service all the equipment they had to move wheat to seaports, which were clogged with ships waiting to load grain for the Soviet Union. A year later, our seaport and railroad facilities were still so strained and busy with hauling Soviet wheat that other vital shipping was being neglected. This sent new shock waves through the economy, and left farmers in grave anxiety about the problems of moving their 1973 harvests to market.

Leftist politicians and consumerists organizing beef boycotts because of high prices did not criticize President Nixon for having caused spiraling food prices, but they did castigate him for not using the force of government to roll them back, or at least freeze them. So Mr. Nixon froze beef prices at the check-out counter, but not at the ranch. The cost of raising beef cattle continued to rise because of the Soviet wheat deal and other government policies. Retail stores could not pay more for beef than they had been paying, because government had frozen their selling prices; and their profit margins were already too slim to be trimmed. With rising costs below, and fixed prices above, the businessmen in the middle (meat packers) were hurt. Giants in the industry might have enough resources to take losses for a while and survive until something favorable happened; but small businesses were soon staggering. Within two weeks after President Nixon froze beef prices, small packers throughout the nation were closing, some never to open again.

Food prices kept rising; so Mr. Nixon froze them all, but left prices of farm products free. Then, cattle feeders could not afford to fatten beef for the market, because feed prices kept rising while beef prices were frozen. Ranchers, for the most part, could hold their cattle; but feeders and more packinghouses were forced to quit. Poultry producers destroyed millions of hatching eggs and baby chicks, because producing chickens for market would cost three times as much as government would allow them to be sold for on the frozen market. Large poultry producers held on, waiting for the government to do something else; but small ones all over the country (and even some rather big ones) closed their businesses.

In the summer of 1973, the House Subcommittee on Agricultural Labor was considering another bill to help out on the farm. This one (H.R. 4011) was called by some of its supporters "a bill of rights for America's farm workers." In fact, it would help the exploiters of farm workers (like Cesar Chavez and the Teamsters Union); but it would be a disaster for farmers.

H. R. 4011 would establish an agricultural labor relations board to regulate the agricultural industry and agricultural labor, in the same way that the National Labor Relations Board regulates labor in other industries. That is, the bill would impose government-supported unionism on American farmers and ranchers and their employees.

Naturally, H.R. 4011 does not prohibit strikes. It provides, however, that once each year a farmer may delay a union strike for 40 days. This is supposed to enable him to get in his harvest before he is struck. But the price he pays for this postponement is high. He must relinquish to an outside arbitrator *full* authority to prescribe a contract between him and the union. Union officials are given a remarkable option. If the *union* likes it, the farmer must accept whatever contract the arbitrator prepares. The union, however, is free to reject the contract and call a strike.

If such a bill ever becomes law, it will create such food shortages and high food prices that America could experience famine for the first time in her history.

Chapter Eight

Federal Form Pollution

MUCH government harassment of producers is muffled in paperwork. Representative H.R. Gross of Iowa says that the major industry of Washington, D.C., is paper shuffling. And how right he is!

One little-discussed aspect of President Nixon's price-control program has been the tremendous burden of paperwork it imposes on businesses, raising their costs while it holds down their selling prices. The first phase of the program went into effect in mid-August of 1971. By the end of the year, the administrative agency, the Cost of Living Council (COLC), was smothering under the mountains of forms it was requiring businesses to fill out and file with Washington. In addition to filing these forms, businesses had to post notices and price schedules and keep records in their stores. Internal Revenue Service agents roamed the land to find out whether businesses were doing the posting and record-keeping required of them; and these IRS investigations required even more filling out and filing of forms in Washington.

On January 15, 1972, COLC eliminated some forms, and reduced the amount of information requested on other forms, for retail firms with less than $200,000 in annual sales. That did not sufficiently abate the paper blizzard. Four days later, COLC totally exempted from controls all retail firms with less than $100,000 a year in sales. At the same time, however, COLC greatly increased the number of forms to be filled out and filed by middle-sized and large businesses. These went into the mails along with threat of "crackdowns" on all businesses that failed to comply promptly. Professional people with payrolls (doctors, lawyers, and others) were warned that they must keep special records always complete and available for review.

When Mr. Nixon's emergency freeze of prices went into effect on June 24, 1973, every merchant in the nation had to post notices and prices in his store and be prepared to furnish to any customer, on demand, a list of legal ceiling prices on all merchandise in the store. On June 25, 1973, a force of 2000 Internal Revenue Agents fanned out over the country making spot checks to see whether merchants were complying.

The paper burden is not a new cross to be borne temporarily while the "emergency" price-control program is in effect. It is a permanent problem that has been going on and growing for decades. Twenty years ago, a Hoover Commission Task Force reported that the government-imposed paper burden was hurting all businesses, and crushing many little ones. The Task Force reported that the owners of some small businesses spent more than one-fourth of their time compiling statistics and filling out forms for the federal government.

Every year, however, Congress creates new federal agencies which fabricate new regulations to control businesses; and every new regulation produces more forms for businessmen to fill out and more reports for them to file. The blizzard of government paperwork relentlessly grows in fury.

The new OSHA agency, as previously indicated, may already have surpassed all others in the overall volume and intensity of its paper bombardment of businessmen; but it is not likely that even OSHA will ever prepare a form to equal a questionnaire mailed out by the Federal Power Commission (FPC) in November, 1963. This FPC document thus far holds the record as the mightiest single paper salvo from the guns of a federal agency. It filled 350 pages 24 inches wide and 14 inches deep. A single copy of it weighed 10 pounds, but it was mailed in 40-pound packages, because each recipient was required to fill it out in quadruplicate. It was accompanied by a 65-page booklet of instructions on how the fill out the form. And all of this was sent to 114 producers of natural gas. Careful estimates of the cost to the individual company of completing the questionnaire ranged as high as $85,000 for salaries alone.

The government paperwork load is heavier for many small businesses than the tax load. In some transactions, real estate firms, large and small, must deal with as many as 25 agencies at various levels of government. In fact, there are some businesses which are potentially subject to the control and ukase of more than 380 separate governmental agencies; and quite often the requirements of one agency, if strictly observed, conflict with the requirements of other agencies.

Moreover, government now forces businesses to hire minority workers who have few if any skills, and then adds to their burden of cost by the paperwork it requires because of such hiring. For example: A Washington, D.C., business concern was accused by the local Equal Employment Opportunity agency of discriminating against Negroes because it was not seeking new employees through the Urban League (a left-wing, tax-exempt Negro organization). The company explained that it did not need the services of the Urban League because it was hiring Negroes by other means. To make the company prove that it was telling the truth, the government agency compelled it to submit copies of all application forms for a three-month period, showing who was hired, who rejected, and why.

Often, the filling out of government forms and questionnaires is not nearly as burdensome as keeping records necessary to produce the information government demands — information that is of no value whatever to the business firm forced to produce it, or to anyone else, except as it may be a useful statistical tool for empire building and power grabbing within the bureaucracy.

In 1972, the Senate Subcommittee on Government Regulations began an investigation of this problem. After holding hearings in only four cities, the chairman of the Subcommittee (Thomas J. McIntyre, D.-N.H.) concluded that "federal-form pollution . . . is strangling small businessmen all across the country."

Every year, American businesses spend 130 million man-hours processing and filing with federal agencies some two billion pieces of paper which occupy about 4.5 million cubic feet of storage space. Senator McIntyre estimates that the over-all cost of this record-keeping and form-filing is $36 billion a year. Half of that ($18 billion a year) is the direct cost to businesses of preparing and filing the federal reports. It costs the federal government (meaning all taxpayers, including businesses) $10 billion a year to print and review the forms which businessmen fill out and file, and $8 billion a year to store them in filing rooms of the federal agencies.

In addition, state and local governments require businesses to file an uncountable welter of reports and forms.

Big business firms hire staffs of persons who work exclusively at keeping records and making reports for governmental agencies. Owners of small businesses, once able to do their own bookkeeping, have been forced by the requirements of government paperwork to get outside professional help. Some very small businessmen, who once could do all the work of running their businesses including the bookkeeping, have become so bogged down in paperwork for the government that they have hired an employee or two to help run the business, so that the owner may have more time for the paperwork. In most of these cases, however, the owner finds that hiring even one employee so increases his paperwork for government that he is worse off than before he hired the help. The Senate Subcommittee interviewed small employers who said: "The cost in time and money is too much. No more employees for us." "Government red tape has made it unprofitable to hire a marginal worker or to go to the expense of training new workers. Paperwork is killing us." "A businessman must risk violating federal law simply because he can't afford the help necessary to keep up."

A typical case: On May 31, 1973, Smith, Burris & Company (an old but small Chicago investment securities firm) went out of business because, the president of the firm said, "Little guys like us can't afford compliance departments to handle all the paperwork and other burdens imposed by various regulatory agencies of government."

Is the general public affected by the paperwork which government forces upon 13.5 million employers? Of course. The general public pays the bill — all $36 billion a year of it.

Chapter Nine

A Can Of
Legal Worms

IN RECENT years, some federal programs,
authorized by Congress for purposes that sound
noble, have operated quite openly as revolutionary efforts to eliminate the free enterprise
system; uproot and overturn established institutions, traditions, and mores of our society; and
convert the federal government into a socialist
dictatorship. And Congress has continued to
fund them with multimillions of dollars of tax
money.

The most notable of such operations have
all been part of the so-called Poverty War — especially the federal Legal Services Program (LSP).

Created ostensibly to give legal aid to the
poor in non-criminal matters, LSP immediately
became a tax-fueled engine for fomenting class
warfare, racial strife, riots, and anarchy as a
means of promoting Marxist revolution in the
United States. The Poverty-War lawyers are not,
in the main, people eager to help the poor. They
are militant leftists hungry for power and bent
on social disruption.

The role of Poverty-War lawyers in creating
Cesar Chavez's United Farm Workers Organizing
Committee to get control of agricultural labor

has already been mentioned. Working closely with the Department of Housing and Urban Development (HUD), the Poverty-War lawyers were also a driving force in organizing (October 1969) a nationwide tenants union, called the National Tenants Organization (NTO). The aim of NTO is to socialize the housing industry in the United States by eliminating private ownership of rented dwellings. The first national director of the tenants union was Anthony R. Henry, a militant Marxist. On October 20, 1969, immediately after NTO was formed, *U.S. News & World Report* quoted Henry as saying that a long-range goal of the union "is to force the federal, state, or local government to take over housing for low and middle-income families where the landlords have failed to operate it properly, or subsidize someone who will operate it properly."

The *force* Mr. Henry speaks of here consists of harassing litigation (performed free for the union by Poverty-War lawyers) and rent strikes (organized and directed for the union by Poverty-War militants) intended to push landlords into bankruptcy, or to demoralize them until they abandon their properties. By *proper operation* of housing Mr. Henry means operation as prescribed by his union officials.

It is easy for vandals, coached and incited by Poverty-War lawyers and union officials, to put rental housing in bad condition overnight. This gives evidence of "improper operation"; it provides a pretext for a rent strike; and when the matter goes to court, it gives Poverty-War lawyers an emotionally appealing argument: The poor tenants are striking, they argue, only because the slumlord will not repair smashed windows, broken doors, mutilated walls, and nonfunctioning plumbing.

The *someone* Henry mentioned, who might be subsidized to operate housing (in lieu of outright government ownership and operation), means either the tenants union or the Welfare Rights Organization (WRO), another Marxist-dominated pressure group organized under the leadership of federal employees in the Departments of HUD and HEW and in Poverty-War organizations. Under rules laid down by the Department of Housing and Urban Development in 1969, and under terms of the Housing and Urban Development Act of 1970, no one (not even local or state governments) can get tax money from Washington to operate federally subsidized housing unless there is "maximum tenant participation" in all aspects of administration, management, and maintenance. "Tenant participation" means participation by an organization representing tenants; and the only organizations that qualify under HUD practices are a tenants union or the Welfare Rights Organization.

Housing for low and middle-income families, mentioned by Anthony Henry, means at least 80 percent of all housing in the United States. Once that much of our housing is socialized, the tax burden on private enterprise to subsidize socialized housing will become so great that private housing for all except the very wealthy, government officials, and union bosses must vanish.

Is it fair to imply that Anthony Henry, speaking in a private capacity as head of a tenants union, was expressing government policy? I think so. A Legal Services Program official in Washington, when asked how the poor would be helped by the bankrupting of landlords with rent strikes, replied that the *government* should provide housing for the poor. And the fact is that Poverty-War attorneys, in helping to organize the National Tenants Organization, were following policy set in Washington, at Cabinet level.

On December 9 and 10, 1966, a Conference on Tenants' Rights was held in Washington, D.C. The Conference was called at the request of President Lyndon Johnson. It was sponsored by Robert C. Weaver, a member of various Communist Fronts, who was then Secretary of Housing and Urban Development; Sargent Shriver, then director of the OEO, and later the Democrat candidate for Vice President; and Ramsey Clark, then Acting Attorney General. A report on the Conference was prepared by Ramsey Clark's Department of Justice and published by the Government Printing Office in 1967. The report is written in the ambiguous dialectic of the Left. Translated into standard English, the report may be summarized as follows:

The Conference suggested that tenants be given *governmental power* to enforce housing code provisions — this to be achieved by organizing tenants into a national union financed with tax money. The Conference acknowledged that, in some areas, Legal Services Program attorneys were already organizing tenants unions and that such activity was illegal under the statute which created LSP. It suggested, however, that the attorneys should continue and that the law should be changed to legalize such activity.

In working to organize a national tenants union, the lawyers of the federal Legal Services Program used tactics officially recommended in *Handbook on Housing Law,* prepared specifically for LSP attorneys with tax money provided by the Office of Economic Opportunity.

The *Handbook* warns LSP attorneys to keep ever in mind that the purpose of organizing a tenants union is not to help poor individuals who may be having housing problems. The objective is to build power for the union. The way to do this is to make tenants dependent on the union. Hence, in cities where a tenants union is organized, federal LSP lawyers are told not to give legal aid in matters concerned with housing to any poor individual without first sending him to the tenants union for clearance. If the union approves (but only if the union approves), LSP may help the poor person who thinks he needs a lawyer.

In helping to organize such radical unions, the

government's Poverty-War lawyers are attacking entire industries. They also attack individual businesses. In this activity, they use the unions they helped to create; but more often they use federal courts for legal harassment of individual businesses.

Individuals and private businesses brought to court by Poverty-War lawyers are at a disadvantage. When someone is sued by *government lawyers*, the public is prone to consider him guilty of something or other, no matter what the disposition of the case. Moreover, an unscrupulous plaintiff, getting legal services free from an unscrupulous lawyer on the federal payroll, can seriously hurt a private business or individual who must pay for legal defense. Even if the lawsuit terminates in favor of the defendant, proving him guiltless, the defendant has been hurt by bad publicity, legal expense, and loss of valuable time.

Such persecution of businessmen has been noticed particularly in California, because an official OEO report (January 1971) gave details on it. This was an evaluation report on California Rural Legal Assistance (CRLA — federal Poverty-War lawyers in rural California), written by Lewis K. Uhler, director of the California Office of Economic Opportunity, after a field investigation. The following are some of the cases Mr. Uhler discussed:

In 1970, Simi Winery, Incorporated, of Healdsburg, California, discharged a vineyard worker for numerous absences from work and for use of intoxicants while on the job. On September 1, 1970, the CRLA filed suit against the company on behalf of the discharged worker, claiming that he had been fired illegally so that the company could hire an alien worker to replace him. Before the company even knew it was being sued, a story appeared in the *Santa Rosa Press Democrat* to the effect that the company was being taken to court for firing workers and replacing them with "wetbacks" (aliens who cross the Mexican border illegally). The allegation against the company was a lie, and judgment in the company's favor was entered on November 19, 1970. Nonetheless, the company had spent $3,700 to defend itself against the suit, and had received a great deal of unfavorable publicity.

In the early summer of 1969, the press of Santa Barbara County featured a story about farm workers who had been seriously injured at the Santa Maria Berry Farms by dangerous pesticides the grower was spraying on his crops. The story said that CRLA had brought suit on behalf of two injured workers against the Santa Maria Berry Farms and the Department of Agriculture. Several lengthy hearings disclosed that the grower had not sprayed pesticides at all, but a harmless fertilizer, and that the two employees who had claimed injuries were not in fact injured. The case was dismissed, *at the request of the director of the CRLA office in Santa Maria.* In asking dismissal, the Poverty-War lawyer said the suit had been filed for the primary purpose of forcing the Agriculture Department to make available its records on pesticide spraying in the county. The OEO report on this case said:

> The suit died with the dismissal, but the damage had been done. The defendants had been forced to defend a costly suit. Equally important, fears and tensions had been stirred in the local citizenry, who believed they were being poisoned by local growers spraying dangerous pesticides. The resentments and hostilities had been fueled between farm workers and their employers, by encouraging the workers to think they were being . . . injured by their employers.

The OEO investigators learned of one case in which CRLA's Poverty-War lawyers brought suit against a local car dealer in Lake County, California, on behalf of 16 Indians. Later, 15 of the Indians gave depositions stating that they had not even been *consulted* before they were made party to the lawsuit. On another occasion, CRLA attorneys in the Salinas office gave union-organizing lessons to nine employees of a certain grower. When the employees were fired for impermissible union activity during working hours, CRLA attorneys brought suit against the grower.

In his evaluation report, Mr. Uhler made this point: "In private litigation, CRLA attorneys do not consider the economic limitations on their opponents. Any one at any time can be their defendant, and they can (and will) pursue their point without regard to economic realities or the underlying merits of the case .... In reality, they [Poverty-War lawyers] are the plaintiffs as well as the attorneys, since they have no economic or other stake and can therefore persist to incredible lengths." Lewis Uhler also reported that CRLA attorneys, whenever possible, filed suits at such times and in such places that they would come before particular federal judges who were "sympathetic to the cause of these attorneys."

And U.S. Representative John R. Rarick says the Poverty War's Legal Services Program "is a subversive movement . . . to redistribute wealth and power as part of a more extensive plan to communize the United States." Richard Buckley, former director of the Legal Services Program in New Orleans, has publicly acknowledged that "Legal Services exist for the redistribution of wealth and power." But the most revealing statement about the federal Poverty-War lawyers is one that a group of them made about themselves in the summer of 1970. Consider:

In June 1970, ten Texas lawyers invited William Kunstler to attend a "Radical Lawyers Caucus" at the Texas State Bar Convention in San Antonio on July 2. Seven of the ten who publicly issued the invitation were LSP lawyers from Dallas — one of the seven being then the director of the Dallas LSP. The *Texas Bar Journal* refused to print an advertisement inviting attorneys to the "Radical Lawyers Caucus." Here are extracts from the advertisement the LSP wanted to run:

Our society is in deep trouble. Well-earned trouble. It is dominating people the world over — because of business investments, military interests, religious intolerance, and racism. At home it is engaged in criminally exploiting black, chicano and other ethnic minorities — because of business's interest in cheap labor, and institutional and individual racism . . . . Even people who are 'making it' are driven to the brink of frustration and alienation — because of society's desire to cling to a humanly useless profit system. Society's supporting institutions and values of religion, the work ethic, puritanism, and self-denial have confused and debased its citizens . . . .

A lack of resources and technology are not the problem, but rather the existing social structures and their by-products: the economic and governmental systems, and the religious, racial and sexual hang-ups . . . .

The hope of the world lies with the groups in motion to basically change society: the students, the blacks, the chicanos, the New Left people in the larger community, and the millions of people in the Third World. The danger comes from those forces in control using the tools of economic, legal and political repression to destroy, imprison and intimidate these groups and individuals . . . .

We lawyers . . . can work to keep radicals from being imprisoned and harassed. We can affirmatively challenge the many institutions being inhumanely used to make people conform . . . .

A major contribution of the Legal Services Program to the war against the social and economic order we call "free enterprise" is the example LSP has set for, and the encouragement it has given to, lawyers to shun normal practice in order to join the New Left radical movement. William Kunstler and many others, campaigning for social disruption and chaos, have carried this LSP message to law students throughout the nation: *Your first commitment is not to the law or to your careers, but to the movement; stay out of conventional practice and join the New Left movement.*

Some have joined. In the June 1970 graduating class of Harvard Law School, there were 37 former editors of the *Harvard Law Review* — regarded as being among the most accomplished and promising of law students. All 37 of them could have stepped into high-income positions with prosperous law firms, but none did. Most went into the Legal Services Program and other branches of government service.

Ralph Nader makes the same plea to young lawyers, somewhat more subtly and possibly more effectively than it is made by men like Kunstler. Nader says: "The best lawyers should be spending their time on the great problems — on water and air pollution, on racial injustice, on juvenile delinquency." In the summer of 1969, Nader asked for 200 volunteers to work at his Center for the Study of Responsive Law. About 4,000 students volunteered, including one-third of the entire student body of Harvard Law School.

Not only law students but many other Americans of diverse occupations and ages regard Nader as a selfless crusader in the noble cause of reform. Some who have watched more carefully believe that he is exploiting legitimate public interest in environment, ecology, safety, and health; that his motivation is a selfish lust for power; and that he intends to use the power he seeks not to reform but to destroy. In 1971, Thomas Shepard Jr., then editor of *Look* magazine, said: "Mr. Nader isn't interested in seeing U.S. industry clean house. What he wants is the entire house, from cellar to attic. His goal is bottom-to-top takeover of industry by government." Paul Rand Dixon, a member of the Federal Trade Commission, has been quoted as saying of Nader: "He's preaching revolution, and I'm scared."

Ralph Nader is not merely preaching revolution. He is helping to create it. He has established several organizations as instrumentalities, covers, and fund-raisers for his activities. All of them enjoy federal tax exemption. They are supported financially by wealthy, tax-exempt foundations — notably, the Carnegie Corporation of New York, the New York Foundation (whose trustees are members of the *New York Times* Sulzberger family), and the New World Foundation (whose board of directors includes Anthony Lewis of the *New York Times*).

The most significant Nader organization is his Center for the Study of Responsive Law, founded in 1968. Another law center incorporated in the same year (and almost exactly like Nader's) is the Center for Law and Social Policy, founded by such persons as Arthur Goldberg (former union attorney, Secretary of Labor,

Supreme Court Justice, and U.S. Ambassador to the United Nations); Stewart Udall (former Secretary of the Interior); and Ramsey Clark (former Attorney General). Like Nader's Center for the Study of Responsive Law, the Center for Law and Social Policy enjoys tax exemption from the federal government and generous financial support from huge tax-exempt foundations, among them the Ford Foundation, Stern Fund, Meyer Fund, and Rockefeller Brothers Fund.

Various officials in these tax-exempt law centers are also officials of organizations enmeshed in the network of organizations interlocked with the Council on Foreign Relations — which for years has operated as the information-and-control center of a complicated conglomerate of tax-exempt groups now constituting an invisible government of the United States.* The same kind of interlock (overlapping of official personnel) exists between the law centers and militant tax-exempt environmental groups. Interlocked with the law centers and environmental groups are law firms enjoying federal tax exemption as "public interest" law firms because they represent environmental groups; and law firms that act as official lobbyists for groups working with environmentalists. Consider a few examples of this complicated interlock:

- Arthur Goldberg and Ramsey Clark, offi-

---

*See Dan Smoot, *The Invisible Government* (Belmont, Mass.: Western Islands, 1965), and Gary Allen, *None Dare Call It Conspiracy* (Seal Beach, Calif.: Concord Press, 1972).

cials of the Center for Law and Social Policy, registered their law firms as lobbyists for the Alaska Federation of Natives, a group which, at the time, was making common cause with environmental groups blocking construction of the Alaska oil pipeline. Lawyers representing the environmental groups were connected with Goldberg and Clark's Center for Law and Social Policy.

● Ramsey Clark is an official of the tax-exempt American Civil Liberties Union (ACLU), which has interlocking connections with the Council on Foreign Relations. The ACLU also represents environmental and "Civil Rights" causes and groups.

● Stewart Udall, of the Center for Law and Social Policy, is a director of the environmental group called the Overview Foundation. The president and treasurer of the Overview Foundation is Henry L. Kimelman, who was national finance chairman for, and the biggest financial contributor to, George McGovern's Presidential campaign in 1972.

● The Washington, D.C., law firm of Mortimer Caplin (former Commissioner of Internal Revenue), enjoying federal tax exemption as a "public interest" firm, represents an environmental group called the National Resources Defense Council.

● Attorneys representing most of the militant environmental groups maintain connection with Ralph Nader's Center for the Study of Responsive Law, or with the Center for Law and Social Policy, or with both.

Not all groups represented by activist lawyers are environmentalists. Many are "equality" groups, whose attacks on society are made under the aegis of various "Civil Rights" laws. Many activist lawyers (representing the National Association for the Advancement of Colored People, the Urban League, the Student Nonviolent Coordinating Committee, and so on) specialize in "Civil Rights" activities and have only occasional connection with environmental and consumerism affairs. And activist lawyers on the federal payroll in the Legal Services Program do not always have direct connections with the private law centers or with environmentalist and consumerist groups.

It sounds like a can of worms, but it works like precision machinery. The law centers recruit lawyers and train them in revolutionary activism. The lawyers then act as legal counsel for militant groups. Together, they have converted lobbying into a sophisticated triple threat, operating in the Legislative, Executive, and Judicial arenas at local, state, and federal levels — although the federal tax code, which gives all of them tax exemption, prohibits lobbying by tax-exempt groups.

In the Legislative arena, activist lawyers and the groups they represent lobby for new laws to punish or control business, alleging that business is trampling on "Civil Rights," or needlessly polluting the environment, or abusing consumers. In the Executive arena, they lobby with, publicly clamor against, and otherwise exert pressure on regulatory agencies to impose harsher controls on business under existing laws. In the Judicial arena, they file lawsuit after lawsuit.

Almost every employer is vulnerable to prosecution for "Civil Rights" violations. The Civil Rights Act of 1964, as amended, prohibits employment practices that discriminate against job-applicants or employees because of race, sex, age, language, religion, or national origin. An employer may not even mention any of these categories in help-wanted ads, employee-recruitment activities, or job applications. Yet the law requires "affirmative action" programs by employers to find, hire, train, and promote "minority" personnel. Under administrative and court interpretation of the "affirmative action" provision, an employer must make the very discriminations that the law prohibits. If not, the Equal Employment Opportunities Commission (EEOC), the administrative agency established by the Civil Rights Act, is likely to find that he does not have the balance of all groups that EEOC thinks desirable. The 1964 Act *requires* private employers to hire and handle employees on the basis of impartial standards applicable to everyone; but the EEOC *prohibits* them from using impartial standards if doing so does not produce the "balance" EEOC wants.

Not giving a woman leave of absence for pregnancy is a discriminatory practice against her because she is a woman. Giving a woman leave of absence for pregnancy is a discriminatory practice against men because they never get

119

such leave. An employer with a policy of hiring new employees recommended by old employees is in violation of the "Civil Rights" laws — *if* a majority of his old employees are white. But if a majority of the old employees are non-white, the employer is urged to hire new employees recommended by the old ones.

No matter how flimsy an alleged grievance may be, any employee who claims that his own "Civil Rights" have been violated (*i.e.,* that he personally has been harmed) by his employer, now has standing to file a federal lawsuit against that employer. An activist lawyer can sometimes incite one or more employees to make such allegations. Then, with clients who have standing to bring legal action, the federal lawyer can file a lawsuit. This does not mean that he always wins the case. Many times, he does not expect to win. Often, as was previously illustrated in the discussion of Poverty-War lawyers in California, lawsuits against employers are filed only to harass, or to serve some agitational or propaganda purpose of the federal lawyers.

Because it is relatively easy for activist lawyers to find clients with standing to file lawsuits against employers under "Civil Rights" statutes, the volume of such cases is rather large. In fiscal 1972, there were 10,436 federal cases against employers for alleged "Civil Rights" violations. Here are some typical cases:

The Supreme Court ruled that an employer may not exclude women and members of minority groups from jobs because they fail to meet routine standards that the company requires of all applicants. The fact that the standards are clearly related to the jobs in question, and are in no way intended to discriminate against anyone except persons unqualified for the jobs, is irrelevant, the court ruled. The court said the standards were discriminatory, because not enough women and minority-group members had met them.

In January 1973, a U.S. Court of Appeals ruled that an employer violates the Civil Rights Act of 1964 if he has a policy of refusing to hire persons with records of frequent arrests. The court said such a policy has the "foreseeable" result of denying Negroes equal opportunity for employment, because Negroes are more likely than whites to have police records.

A company refused to hire an experienced woman welder because it did not have separate toilet and locker-room facilities for women. Since employers are prohibited from making any distinction between the sexes, the employer was in violation of the "Civil Rights" laws by even considering the problem of separate facilities for women. The EEOC overlooked the law, however. It held the employer in violation of the woman's "Civil Rights" because he refused to hire her, and ordered the employer to provide separate facilities for her (in violation of the law) — saying the cost to the employer would not be prohibitive.

A radio station which hired only male newscasters because its listening audience preferred to listen to men was held in violation of the Civil Rights Act.

Male employees of the Bank of America in San Francisco complained to management that they were being discriminated against because the bank was paying taxicab fares for women who worked nights, but was not doing the same for men on the same shifts. The bank stopped providing the special benefit for women. When male employees made a similar complaint against Pacific Telephone and Telegraph Company, the company rejected their complaint. The male employees filed a "Civil Rights" lawsuit against the company — which continued giving its women taxi fare pending the outcome of the case.

Action in court against government agencies, charging them, in effect, with coddling leniency toward business, has had a far more damaging effect on business, and on society in general, than has direct litigation against individual businesses. Such cases have been relatively limited in number, however, because the activists could not always show that they had standing to file such cases. The old Administrative Procedure Act (1946) gives any individual the necessary standing to sue a federal agency (with some specific exceptions and limitations) *if* the individual alleges that he was personally harmed by the agency's action. An individual cannot sue a federal agency merely because he dislikes what the agency did or, in a general way, thinks it bad for the country.

The case of *Sierra Club v. Morton* illustrates the point. The Sierra Club brought suit, asking a U.S. District Court to restrain the Department of the Interior from granting permits for a proposed Walt Disney Enterprises development of a commercial skiing resort in the Mineral King Valley section of Sequoia National Forest. The Club brought action under the Administrative Procedure Act of 1946, but did not allege injury to the Club itself or to any of its members. The lawsuit alleged that the skiing project would change the aesthetics and ecology of a natural resource. The Club claimed that its expertise in such matters gave it standing, as a "representative of the public," to bring the lawsuit. The District Court granted a preliminary injunction.

The Department of the Interior appealed, and the U.S. Appellate Court reversed the lower court, saying the Sierra Club lacked standing to bring the suit, because it had not shown, or claimed, injury to itself or its members. The Club appealed. The U.S. Supreme Court (in a 4-3 decision, Justices Lewis F. Powell Jr. and William H. Rehnquist not participating) upheld the Appellate Court. Justice Potter Stewart wrote the majority opinion, saying that the Sierra Club lacked standing to seek judicial review in this case because it "failed to allege that it or its members would be affected in any of their activities or pastimes by the Disney development." Mr. Justice Stewart said that "the principle that the Sierra Club would have us establish in this case" would "authorize judicial review at the behest of organizations or individuals who seek to do no more than vindicate their own value preferences through the judicial process."

In a footnote, however, Mr. Justice Stewart virtually invited the Sierra Club to amend its complaint in District Court, and thus initiate another lawsuit, claiming damage to itself or members. The Club refused the invitation. Apparently the Sierra Club and its lawyers were not primarily interested in winning this one case. Rather, they wanted to set, in our country's highest court, a precedent which would give the Club and similar groups almost limitless latitude to supervise economic activities of private business by bringing lawsuits against federal agencies with whom businesses must deal.

Justice William O. Douglas agreed with the Sierra Club's activist lawyers. Dissenting in *Sierra Club v. Morton*, Douglas said: "These environmental issues should be tendered by the inanimate object itself. Then there will be assurances that all forms of life which it [the Supreme Court] represents will stand before the court — the pileated woodpecker as well as the coyote and bear, the lemmings as well as the trout in the streams."

Conceding that the ideal of allowing woodpeckers, coyotes, bears, lemmings, and fish to bring suit in federal court is beyond reach, Mr. Justice Douglas suggested what he considers the next best thing: allow environmental enthusiasts unlimited standing to bring federal lawsuits on behalf of the woodpeckers and coyotes. Douglas said: "Those inarticulate members of the ecological group cannot speak. But those people who have so frequented the place as to know its values and wonders will be able to speak for the entire ecological community."

Would Mr. Justice Douglas include lumbermen and miners among "those people who have so frequented the place as to know its values and wonders," and give them the extraordinary privilege of using the federal courts to challenge any and all federal action regarding federal lands? Of course not. Douglas would give this privilege only to those who share Douglas' viewpoint.

To the surprise of some observers, Justice Harry A. Blackmun (a Nixon appointee, widely advertised as a conservative constitutionalist) joined the Douglas dissent in *Sierra Club v. Morton*. He suggested that the Supreme Court should permit "imaginative expansion of our traditional concepts of standing in order to enable an organization such as the Sierra Club . . . to litigate environmental issues." And Mr. Justice Blackmun added: "We need not fear that Pandora's box will be opened or that there will be no limit to the number of those who desire to participate in environmental litigation. The courts will exercise appropriate restraints just as they have exercised them in the past . . . . And Mr. Justice Douglas, in his eloquent opinion, has imaginatively suggested another means . . . with obvious, appropriate, and self-imposed limitations as to standing . . . that is, that the litigant be one who speaks knowingly for the environmental values he asserts."

Militant activists have also been working in the Legislative arena to obtain for themselves the special privilege of unlimited standing to bring lawsuits that would not merely control, but bankrupt, private businesses in the United States.

About the time Ralph Nader established his Center for the Study of Responsive Law (1968), he organized teams of "Nader's Raiders," whose major task was agitation for a law to permit class-action lawsuits to be brought in federal courts against business firms. Monopolistic unions and other "consumer advocates" supported Nader's efforts. The law Nader demanded would permit any group of consumers, no matter how small, to file federal lawsuits against business firms on the basis of simple allegations that the consumers had been harmed by some practice of the firms. The consumers could share lawyers' fees and court costs. If they won their case, the businesses would have to pay them damages and reimburse them for all their legal expense; and every other similarly affected consumer in the United States, though not a party to the suit, could also collect damages. Nader also wanted consumer groups given unlimited standing to strike at business by filing lawsuits against federal agencies dealing with businesses, and by intervening in cases in controversy between federal agencies and businesses.

On October 30, 1969, President Nixon sent

Congress a packet of proposed laws which, he said, would create "a comprehensive program of consumer protection." Congress enacted none of these laws. On September 11, 1970, Mr. Nixon renewed his demand for the consumer-protection bills, criticizing Congress for inaction. One of the President's consumer-protection bills would, he said, "create for the first time on a national basis a cause of action in Federal courts in cases of unfair and deceptive practices without regard to the amount in controversy."

Three class-action-lawsuit bills were seriously considered in 1970, but none passed. Committee witnesses favoring such legislation displayed the bitter anti-business bias epitomized by Herbert S. Deneberg (Wharton School of Finance, University of Pennsylvania), who testified: "The marketplace inflicts mass fraud and abuse on the consumer." Some witnesses against the legislation, especially representatives of trade associations, committed the moral and tactical error that has long been typical of many "conservative" business groups: although knowing it to be evil, they supported the Nixon proposal, or something like it, because it was less evil than other proposals. No witness arguing against class-action-lawsuit legislation so much as observed that it is unconstitutional, as it clearly is.

Several witnesses, however, forthrightly testified against such legislation on the ground that it is pragmatically wrong. They pointed out that the innocent would be punished instead of the guilty. Illegitimate business firms that engage in fraudulent practices would seldom be sued, they said, because, being illegitimate, these firms seldom have tangible resources that can be seized for payment of damages even if lawsuits against them are successful; but reputable firms guilty of no misbehavior would be sued by lawyers and clients hoping to harass and profit. The witnesses observed that the cost of defending a class-action suit would be backbreaking even for big business, overwhelming for small ones.

As Milton Handler, law professor at Columbia University, said of this legislation: "It invites the consumer to seek damages willy-nilly, in crowded federal courts. Businessmen would be forced to settle rather than risk bankruptcy, in an effort to prove their innocence. This, to me, is little more than the legitimization of legal blackmail."

Herbert H. Schiff of the American Retail Federation testified: "Class actions are harsh and vindictive because of the great recoveries possible against reputable business. Class action defendants are generally not selected on the basis of their guilt, but rather on their ability to pay substantial damages. The determination to sue is placed in the hands of a private attorney who personally benefits from the litigation."

George P. Lamb of the Association of Home Appliance Manufacturers testified: "Class suits will not give effective relief for such business practices as [those complained of] . . . because the defendants are usually not available or are judgment proof . . . . Most illegal practices cited as creating a need for consumer class suits are illegal by state law."

But, Mr. Businessman, if the President has his way, you will soon be facing exactly such class-action suits.

Chapter Ten

The Price Of 600 Birds

In 1966, the Interior Department auctioned off to private oil companies 72 leases in the Santa Barbara Channel — deriving therefrom a net revenue to the federal government totaling $623 million. On January 28, 1969, a Union Oil Company well on a lease off the coast of Santa Barbara blew out. In ten days, before the well could be controlled, it poured some 235,000 gallons of oil into the Pacific Ocean, fouling about 30 miles of beach, damaging boats and wildlife.

President Nixon deplored this accident and appointed a Presidential task force to investigate. On February 7, Secretary of the Interior Walter J. Hickel suspended all drilling and pumping operations in the Santa Barbara Channel. On February 17, Secretary Hickel announced new regulations for drilling on offshore federal leases; and on February 27, he said Union Oil could resume drilling in the Santa Barbara Channel. He was summoned before the Senate Public Works Committee that same day to defend his decision.

In June 1969, President Nixon's task force filed a report concluding that the only way to prevent further leaks in the Santa Barbara Channel was to pump the field dry. Secretary Hickel said he was authorizing resumption of unlimited drilling in the Channel by all oil companies with leases.

Lawsuits filed in federal District Courts sought injunctions against this action by the Interior Secretary. The District Courts refused to issue the injunctions, and the cases (*County of Santa Barbara v. Malley* and *Gulf Oil v. Morton*) were appealed. The Supreme Court upheld the lower courts. Then the Nixon Administration reversed itself and voluntarily imposed a moratorium on all drilling on federal leases in the Santa Barbara Channel. Oil companies affected sued the government, and won in federal District Court. The Nixon Administration appealed, and continued the moratorium, while the litigation moved toward the Supreme Court. Four and a half years later (June 23, 1973), the head of the American Petroleum Institute cited as a major cause of the current fuel shortage the fact that half of the Santa Barbara Channel production was still shut down as a result of the 1969 oil spill. That shortage, however, was not the major result of the spill.

The Santa Barbara Channel oil spill was not an ecological disaster. However, organized environmental groups wanted the nation to think it was; and that is the way the mass media reported it − as if with the purpose of working the public into a frenzy of hatred for the oil industry. Day after day, for many days, the entire nation was shown — via television, news-papers, and magazines — pictures of oil-coated wildfowl on beaches, presumably near Santa Barbara. Commentators on the national net-works routinely referred to the "hundreds of thousands" of birds that were killed. More than four years later, they were still using that round figure. In mid-June 1973, when there were oil slicks in the Santa Barbara Channel from natural seepage having nothing to do with drilling activities — seepage such as had always occurred from time to time in that area, even before offshore oil drilling began — network com-mentators reminded the public of the "hundreds of thousands of birds" killed there by the oil-well blowout in January 1969. But what was the truth? On page 86 of a special study entitled *Energy Crisis in America*, published in 1973, the tediously factual *Congressional Quarterly* says that "an estimated 600 birds were affected by the oil" from the 1969 spill in the Santa Barbara Channel.

The false propaganda was effective, none-theless. In the month following the Santa Barbara "ecological disaster," Senator Henry M. Jackson (D.-Wash.) introduced a bill to establish a national policy on environmental protection, and to set up in the office of the President a Council on Environmental Quality. Jackson had been trying in vain since 1967 to get such legislation passed. But in 1969 for the first time, primarily because of the "disaster," Jackson's bill met no opposition in either House of

Congress. Action on it was slowed down only by a jurisdictional dispute between Senator Jackson (Chairman of the Senate Interior and Insular Affairs Committee) and Senator Edmund S. Muskie (D.-Me., Chairman of the Senate Public Works Subcommittee), each Senator seeking political credit for being the bill's chief sponsor.

President Nixon wanted credit too. Not waiting for legislative authorization that Congress was obviously about to give, the President issued an Executive Order on May 29, 1969, creating a Cabinet-level Environmental Quality Council — to work against increasing threats to "the availability of good air and good water, of open space and even quiet neighborhoods."

The Jackson-Muskie-Dingell environmental bill (Representative John D. Dingell, D.-Mich., being the chief sponsor in the House) was officially styled the National Environmental Policy Act of 1969. It was given unanimous approval by both Houses of Congress late in December. On New Year's Day, 1970, in a special White House ceremony that was supposed to have symbolic significance, President Nixon signed the National Environmental Policy Act (Public Law 91-190), proclaiming it the first official action of the federal government in the new decade of the Seventies.

This law declares it to be the continuing policy of the federal government "to use all practicable means and measures, including financial and technical assistance, in a manner calculated to foster and promote the general welfare, to create and maintain conditions under which man and nature can exist in productive harmony, and fulfill the social, economic, and other requirements of present and future generations of Americans." To implement this policy, the law:

• Called upon local and state governments to cooperate with the federal government to protect the environment.

• Directed agencies of the federal government to consider environmental factors in decision-making.

• Directed that federal agencies include in every recommendation or report on proposals for legislation, and other major federal actions affecting the environment, a statement on the environmental impact of the proposed action, and a statement on possible alternatives.

• Directed all federal agencies to determine by July 1, 1971, whether their policies were in compliance with the purposes of the Act.

• Established in the office of the President a three-member Council on Environmental Quality, to assist the President in the preparation of an annual report on the environment, to review federal activities affecting natural resources, and to conduct studies on the environment.

• Authorized expenditures for the Council of up to $300,000 for fiscal 1970, $700,000 for fiscal 1971, and one million dollars a year thereafter.

• Directed the President (beginning July 1,

1970) to submit an annual Environmental Quality Report to Congress.

At first glance, it sounds well-meaning and harmless; and, as federal expenditures of tax money go, it costs little — only a million dollars a year. But it was a sleeper, as activist attorneys exultantly called it after it was safely on the statute books. This legislation provided the activists with legal standing to make court attacks against major business activities throughout the United States — almost as potent a weapon against business as the activists have been seeking in their demands for legislation authorizing "consumer protection" and class-action lawsuits.

The environmental-policy law left the definition of environment so vague and open-ended that it gave federal courts almost limitless power to veto the actions of Executive agencies and the laws of Congress. No business can initiate a major activity without first dealing with a government agency of some kind — about permits, licenses, right-of-way leases, land leases, use of public thoroughfares, and so on. Any group of two or more people willing to post a small bond and engage an attorney can bring court action against a governmental agency, alleging that, in granting permission for a business activity, the agency failed to file an adequate environmental-impact statement as required by the National Environmental Policy Act of 1969. They can demand a court injunction to halt the business activity until the government agency files an adequate impact statement and suggests an alternative approach.

Looking upon the law as almost too good to be true from their viewpoint, activist lawyers admit that it probably would not have passed if all Members of Congress who voted for it had known what they were doing — if they had realized what broad, undefined powers they were granting to the courts and, through the courts, to activist lawyers and the small militant groups they represent.

By the end of 1971, more than 160 cases brought under the 1969 law by activist lawyers for environmentalist groups were pending in federal courts. In the previous 182 years of our history — from 1789 to the end of 1971 — the U.S. Supreme Court had heard only four environmental-type cases, all brought by state governments. Three of these had involved charges against other governments (local or state) for polluting waterways with sewage, and one had involved state charges against a business firm for polluting the atmosphere (*Missouri v. Illinois and the Sanitary District of Chicago*, 1906; *New York v. New Jersey*, 1921; *New Jersey v. New York*, 1931; *Georgia v. Tennessee Copper Company*, 1907).

The National Environmental Policy Act has been a breeder of other laws, federal and state. As required by the environmental law, the Council on Environmental Quality made its first annual report on August 10, 1970. It urged

Congress to enact President Nixon's anti-pollution bills. This provided major impetus for the Clean-Air Amendments Act of 1970 and the Clean-Water Act of 1972 — the harshest, most far-reaching, most expensive anti-pollution bills yet enacted. Both of these laws specifically give citizens or groups legal standing (with some limitations) to bring federal lawsuits against businesses and federal agencies alleged to be polluters of the environment.

In consequence of the National Environmental Policy Act of 1969, the California State Legislature enacted the Environmental Act of 1970. This law required California state agencies to prepare environmental-impact statements before initiating government projects.

In September 1972, the California State Supreme Court handed down a decision under the law, holding that state and local agencies cannot approve *private* construction projects whose effects on the environment would be "significant" or "non-trivial" without first preparing and filing an environmental-impact statement and proposing measures to reduce any anticipated adverse effects of the private construction projects in question. The court did not define "significant" and "non-trivial."

Providing undefined authority for state and local agencies to deny building permits, and virtually inviting environmentalist suits challenging new private construction, the court decision dealt the construction industry a stunning blow whose reverberations were felt throughout the economy of California.

State agencies did not know which private building projects would require environmental-impact statements; hence there were costly delays by local governmental and state agencies in issuing permits for private businesses to start new building projects. The court decision also made the financing of proposed private projects quite difficult — impossible in some cases, because lending agencies feared to risk money on projects that might later be crippled by adverse governmental rulings, or by citizens' lawsuits brought on environmental grounds.

In November 1972, the California Supreme Court upheld its own September ruling. The Court refused to define the terms "significant" and "non-trivial," but did, rather testily, say "common sense" would indicate that the majority of projects requiring building permits obviously are exempt from the requirement for filing an environmental-impact statement because they are minor in scope.

That gave state and local agencies, private builders, and lending institutions courage to go ahead with their work, although it still left private builders and their financial backers at the mercy of state agencies, which could refuse permits or impose unreasonable stipulations on environmental grounds — and at the mercy of courts hearing lawsuits brought by environmentalist groups.

Used in conjunction with the National Environmental Policy Act of 1969, the Clean-Air Amendments Act of 1970 and the Clean-Water Act of 1972 enable radical environmentalists to use federal power against businesses within all states in somewhat the same way they can use state power in California under the state's Environmental Quality Act. Under the Clean-Air Amendments Act of 1970, and regulations issued by the Environmental Protection Agency (EPA – the general regulatory agency in the environmental field, created by Presidential Executive Order December 2, 1970), state governments are *required* to achieve federal clean-air standards by 1975, and to formulate and enforce environment-protecting standards within "a reasonable time."

On January 31, 1973, a U.S. Court of Appeals in Washington, D.C., handed down a decision in a lawsuit brought by the environmental group called National Resources Defense Council. The court said states must make sure that air-quality standards are maintained, once they are achieved. To carry out the requirements of this decision, the Environmental Protection Agency reviewed the clean-air plans for all 50 states, finding that none of them had made adequate provisions to keep the air clean. Consequently, on April 18, 1973, the EPA proposed a new regulation. All states must review and control any new construction project to make sure that it does not cause a violation of air standards, "either directly, because of emissions from it, or indirectly, because of emissions resulting from mobile source activities associated with it."

For example, a shopping center or drive-in theater may not, of itself, emit enough pollution to be illegal, but the cars that congregate because of it may. The new EPA regulations say that states, before permitting construction projects, must take such circumstances into consideration, reviewing not only the construction plans but also information on operational patterns, "anticipated numbers of employees and/or patrons, expected transportation routes, and habits of employees and/or patrons."

The court set August 15, 1973, as the deadline for EPA to issue clean-air plans for every state which had not, by that time, submitted a plan that would meet clean-air standards requested by one little environmental group, the National Resources Defense Council. Since the automobile is generally blamed for most air pollution, there is no way to meet the clean-air standards environmentalists demand without reducing vehicle pollution. In the short time allowed by the court, there was no way to effect the reduction required except by reducing the use of cars.

Consequently, in the first week of July 1973, the EPA announced a variety of plans, to be imposed in various ways in different areas. They included limiting gasoline sales; prohibiting construction of new parking facilities; compulsory reduction in use of existing off-street parking space; outlawing on-street parking; banning certain types of vehicles from certain places at specific times; imposing penalties on motorists who allow car motors to idle more than five minutes at a time; requiring filling stations to reduce evaporation of gasoline by installing vapor-control systems (at an average cost of $5,000 per station, the cost to be passed on to consumers at the rate of about $3 per car per year); and, as EPA administrator Robert W. Fri put it, other "drastic measures to curtail auto traffic." Mr. Fri said that, under the court order and the clean-air law, he had to impose the plans, regardless of consequences.

These controls over businesses and over people and their activities by governments at all levels throughout the United States are sufficient to raise serious doubts about the survival of our free society — a big price to pay for the death or harming of 600 birds. But the nation will have to pay an even bigger price — much bigger. Government, and organized environmentalists with government help, are raining heavy blows upon business in general. But they plan to do more than that to the one business essential to all others — essential to life as we know it in the United States: the business of producing energy fuels. The foes of this business are preparing for it the *coup de grâce.* They aim to kill it.

Chapter Eleven

Yardsticks And Clubs

ENERGY IS the lifeblood of industrialized nations. Without it, most other resources are useless. Without energy to run its machines; to light and heat its homes, factories, schools, churches, hospitals, offices, and stores; to till its lands and process the products of its farms, mines, and factories; to remove and dispose of its wastes; and to provide transportation for both products and people — an industrialized nation will quickly die.

The United States is the most industrialized of nations. Our economy — our way of life — is built on cheap energy-fuel, abundantly available. We have been spending less than 5 percent of our national income on fuels to produce the energy that gives life to everything else — far less than the cost of energy to any other industrialized nation. Consequently, with only 6 percent of the world's population, we use about 34 percent of all energy produced in the world; and the consequence of that fact is a general, widespread prosperity previously unknown in the history of civilization.

This does not mean, however, that we have been squandering our energy-fuel resources recklessly, using them up faster than was safe. We have — *still* have — within our national jurisdiction enough energy-fuel resources to last us more than a thousand years.

The U.S. Geological Survey estimates that, at current rates of consumption, we have a 500-year supply of petroleum and a 300-year supply of natural gas in the outer continental shelf of our Atlantic, Gulf of Mexico, and Pacific coasts, in Alaska, and in deep mainland fields. We have enough coal reserves to last 1500 years. We have the capacity and necessary raw materials to produce an almost inexhaustible supply of nuclear energy. In a few of our western states, some of the heat stored in the earth is near the surface and available for the production of geothermal energy. Government geologists estimate that, on land owned mostly by the federal government in three western states (Colorado, Utah, and Wyoming), there are two trillion barrels of high-grade oil in shale rock — an amount six times greater than all proved reserves of crude petroleum on earth.

Yet, by the end of the 1960's, we were already critically dependent on foreign sources of supply for a substantial portion of the energy fuels we were using; and our dependence was growing with every month.

Practically all our foreign imports of fuel oil were coming from ten nations — six of them on the Persian Gulf, two in North Africa, two in the Western Hemisphere (Canada and Venezuela). Venezuela's developed reserves were known to be declining, and there were clear signs that Canada was on the verge of restricting crude-oil exports to the United States. This meant a rapidly growing dependence on supplies from eight small nations of the Middle East and North Africa.

Traditionally, the people and governments of that area had been friendly toward America and Americans. But the foreign policies of our government have converted friendliness into hostility. The leading role the United States played in setting up the nation of Israel in the heart of the Arab homeland; the rivers of American money pouring in to arm Israel and keep her socialist economy moving; the publicly announced promises of American Presidents of both major political parties to defend Israel with arms and money (and troops if necessary), no matter the circumstances or the consequences — these activities and policies of the U.S. Government have driven Arab nations into the Communist camp.

It was after this situation had been created that fabulous oil fields in North Africa and on the Persian Gulf were explored and developed — in large part by American expertise, technology, equipment, and money. This phenomenon was also caused by policies of the United States Government that decreased incentives for costly exploration and development in the United States and encouraged investments in cheap foreign production — especially in "backward" or "emerging" nations, and most especially in

144

the Middle East and North Africa, where the U.S. Government seemed to be trying to buy back the friendship which its pro-Israel, anti-Arab foreign policies had sacrificed. In the decade of the 1960's alone, the United States petroleum industry spent almost six times as much on exploration, development, and production abroad as it spent at home.

Our growing dependence on foreign oil was not only making us subject to political blackmail by hostile rulers of oil-producing nations, but was also aggravating our mushrooming balance-of-payments deficits. Purchases of foreign oil by the United States — about $2 billion in 1969 — will total $7 billion in 1973, and are expected to reach $13 billion a year by 1975 and $31 billion annually by 1985.

There, hastily sketched, is the picture confronting our country at the end of 1969. For oil, the lifeblood of our industrialized civilization, we were sinking into hopeless dependence upon eight small nations in an area where hatred of the United States had become a major article of faith with the people, a powerful political tool for the governments.

Yet at the end of 1969 (largely because 600 birds had been affected by an oil-well blowout in the Santa Barbara Channel), Congress enacted the National Environmental Policy Act. Within 18 months that law had been responsible for stopping the building of nuclear power plants; for preventing oil exploration on the outer-continental shelf; for sharply curtailing oil production in offshore fields already explored and tapped; for prohibiting the building of the Alaska pipeline; for preventing the leasing of oil-shale lands; and for reducing the production of coal.

In September 1970, President Nixon told the Economic Club of Detroit: "We are not going to allow the environmental issue . . . to destroy the industrial system that made this the great country it is."

Nine months before making that statement, the President, with a considerable fanfare of publicity, had signed not only the environmental law but also the restrictive Federal Coal Mine Health and Safety Act of 1969. Three months after his Detroit speech, the President (with more fanfare) signed the clean-air law of 1970. The impact of those three federal laws, and action by environmentalists, have gone a long way toward allowing "the environmental issue . . . to destroy the industrial system that made this the great country it is." The domestic production of energy was further, and severely, reduced as a result of these laws, while consumption of energy was greatly increased.

NUCLEAR ENERGY

In his first energy message to Congress (June 4, 1971), President Nixon called nuclear power "our best hope for meeting the nation's growing demand for economical clean energy." Authorities on nuclear power and advocates of its development have held out this bright promise for more than 25 years.

The first full-scale commercial nuclear power plant went into operation in 1957 at Shippingport, Pennsylvania. It is a 90,000-watt facility, owned jointly by the Duquesne Light Company and the Atomic Energy Commission (AEC). By the end of 1970, 22 nuclear power plants were in operation; 55 were under construction; 44 were being designed.

But in 1971, small groups of militant environmentalists brought the construction of nuclear power plants to a virtual standstill. Their activist lawyers used provisions of the National Environmental Policy Act of 1969 to get federal court injunctions against the operation of nuclear plants on grounds that the Atomic Energy Commission had issued licenses without filing adequate environmental-impact statements.

Moved by the gravity of the situation, Congress passed Public Law 92-307 on May 17, 1972, authorizing the AEC to issue temporary operating licenses for certain nuclear power plants whose operation was necessary to ensure an adequate power supply, and whose application for full operating licenses had been challenged. This applied to about 13 plants whose applications for licenses were being held up because of attacks by environmentalists. But Congress rendered the law practically useless as a means of expediting the construction of nuclear power plants by adding a provision (opposed by both the AEC and the power industry) requiring public hearings before the temporary licenses could be issued. With their well-financed lawyers, the tax-exempt environmental groups can convert public hearings into time-consuming, tax-dollar-eating legal harangues that are almost as effective as court injunctions in blocking action.

Environmentalists have attacked nuclear power plants for thermal pollution — discharging warm water into streams. They claim this may have a harmful effect on wildlife, especially fish, which may not be able to adapt to the change in water temperature. For example, when a utility firm in New Jersey temporarily shut down a nuclear power plant for minor repairs, environmentalists attacked the company, saying that fish in an adjacent creek had hung around instead of migrating southward because they liked the warm water caused by the plant's discharge. When the plant shut down, the fish were caught unawares in cooler water than they had come to like.

Environmentalists also claim to fear the possibility of transportation accidents while nuclear fuel and radioactive wastes are being transported to and from plants. The AEC and industry guard carefully against such accidents, and there has never been one in which people were injured as a result of the radioactivity of the contents of the shipment.

Environmentalists say nuclear power plants leak harmful amounts of radiation. The AEC points out that in AEC's 16 years of operating experience no one has ever been injured by radiation from any commercial reactor.

The environmentalists' loudest objection to nuclear power plants is that a freak accident in a plant *could have* cataclysmic consequences in the surrounding community — and perhaps far beyond. They ignore the fact that the AEC and industry take elaborate precautions and have required every possible safeguard against freak accidents, with the result that none has ever occurred.

Nonetheless, the development of more nuclear power is still trammeled by environmental lawsuits brought by activist lawyers using government to strangle the energy American business needs not only to grow but to survive.

SHALE OIL

In 1969, Walter J. Hickel (then Secretary of the Interior) appointed a three-man task force to study the problem of developing oil from shale on government lands. The task force recommended leasing land for commercial development. On May 18, 1970, however, Secretary Hickel notified a Senate subcommittee on fuels that his Department had decided to "delay its decision" on leasing shale lands, because "it would be premature, for economic reasons, to go ahead with oil shale development."

Secretary Hickel's notice was puzzling. Recent testimony by Interior Department officials had assured Congress that development of oil-shale deposits was urgently needed for economic reasons. Moreover, no expenditure of tax money or granting of special privilege to business was involved. The government would merely sell leases on a competitive-bid basis to businesses, which would not only pay for the leases but would also provide private capital for the research and development necessary to produce oil from shale. Such leasing, far from causing any economic problem for the government, would bring it immediate revenue from the leases and potentially a very great deal of revenue from shale-oil production.

Fred J. Russell, Under Secretary of the Interior, said Hickel's decision had actually been made for ecological reasons. Leasing of oil-shale lands must be delayed until an environmental-impact study and report could be issued, as required by the National Environmental Policy Act of 1969. More than a year later, with the energy crisis mounting fast, the impact report was still somewhere in the future.

On June 4, 1971, President Nixon sent to Congress the first Presidential message ever to deal with the nation's energy needs. He said: "Over half of our Nation's remaining oil and gas resources, about 40 percent of our coal and uranium, 80 percent of our oil shale, and some 60 percent of our geothermal energy sources are now located on Federal lands. Programs to make these resources available . . . are essential if shortages are to be averted. Through appropriate leasing programs, the Government should be able to recover the fair market value of these resources, while requiring developers to comply with requirements that will adequately protect the environment."

Concerning shale-oil production in particular, the President said:

> At a time when we are facing possible energy shortages, it is reassuring to know that there exists in the United States an untapped shale oil resource containing some 600 billion barrels in high-grade deposits. At current consumption rates, this resource represents 150 years' supply. About 80 billion barrels of this shale oil are particularly rich and well situated for early development. This huge resource of very low sulfur oil is located in the Rocky Mountain area, primarily on Federal land.
>
> At present there is no commercial production of shale oil. A mixture of problems — environmental, technical and economic — have combined to thwart past efforts at development . . . .
>
> I am . . . requesting the Secretary of the Interior to expedite the development of an oil shale leasing program including the preparation of an environmental impact statement. If after reviewing this statement and comments he finds that environmental concerns can be satisfied, he shall then proceed with the detailed planning. This work would also involve the States of Wyoming, Colorado, and Utah and the first test lease would be scheduled for next year.

Now, two years later, no environmental-impact statement about shale-oil development has yet been made public.

COAL

Coal is our most abundant fossil fuel. For a century or more it was the primary energy fuel

151

in use, and we still have enough reserves to last us about 1500 years. Yet coal now provides only 18 percent (or less) of all energy produced in the United States. The coal industry is in bad financial condition — so bad, in fact, that the biggest coal companies have sold out in recent years to oil firms and conglomerates.

Coal's major economic difficulties were caused by government. First, if not foremost, there is the question of labor. Management cannot make coal competitive with other major energy fuels if it does not cut selling prices. It cannot cut selling prices if it cannot cut production costs. It cannot cut production costs unless it can reduce the cost of labor, which accounts for 80 percent of the total cost of producing coal.

Significant reductions in labor costs of producing coal could be achieved without reducing the wages of coal miners. If management in the industries that produce and distribute coal were allowed to manage, it could eliminate useless jobs now occupied by high-paid employees who contribute little or nothing to productivity. Management could then get a good day's work for a good day's pay from employees (thus vastly increasing per-man-hour production and comparably decreasing over-all production costs) by hiring, firing, raising, promoting, or demoting its workers on the basis of their worth to the company. This would get rid of drones and greatly benefit not only management but also all the productive employees. But management in the coal industry, as in the railroad industry to which it is tied, cannot manage. It cannot take either these or any other sensible measures to reduce production and transportation costs, because government has given unions monopolistic control of virtually all labor that goes into the production and distribution of coal.

By 1954, when the federal government imposed price controls on natural gas, the coal industry was no longer able to compete. The Federal Trade Commission had set unreasonably low prices on natural gas. Throughout the United States, where natural gas was available, major energy-fuel users switched from coal to gas.

The Federal Coal Mine Health and Safety Act of 1969 was a more recent blow to the coal industry. Meeting requirements of this law cost coal companies more than a billion dollars and drastically cut already-low worker productivity in underground mines; but it did not make coal mining safer or more salubrious.

The Clean-Air Amendments Act of 1970 set air standards requiring users of high-sulfur coal to eliminate by 1975 emissions of sulfur oxides that result from burning such coal. Industry had been working on this problem for a long time, and had made progress, but not enough. Habitually working on a low profit margin, and recently saddled with a billion-dollar burden by the 1969 health and safety law, the coal industry could not finance a crash program of research and development to make its high-sulfur product acceptable by 1975. The users of coal were in no position to pay for such an undertaking. So the clean-air law eliminated the market for coal with a high sulfur content. Most electric power plants and big industrial installations east of the Mississippi River switched from coal to low-sulfur oil (already in short supply) as boiler fuel. Many big users who could not get such oil — or make the changes necessary to use it — demanded low-sulfur coal, which is obtainable in immense quantities by strip mining.

Strip mining is more efficient, requires much less manpower, and is safer than deep underground mining. For example, in 1970 the average per-man-per-day production from strip mines was 35 tons, as compared with 14 tons from deep mines. Moreover, strip mining does not require the huge capital investments and the long lead time before starting operations that are typical for underground mines. The consequence of these differences is dramatically illustrated by the price of coal. In 1970, stripped coal sold for $4.69 a ton, deep-mined coal for $7.40 a ton.

The coal industry turned to strip mining. In 1971, for the first time in history, surface mining surpassed underground mining as a method of coal production. In 1971 and 1972, nearly 850 underground coal mines closed.

The U.S. Bureau of Mines estimates that there are more than a trillion tons of low-sulfur coal in four western states: Montana, Wyoming, North Dakota, and South Dakota — a great deal of it on land owned by the federal government. The Bureau says about 35 billion tons of this vast reserve is "economically strippable," most of it lying just below the surface in seams 50 to 200 feet thick.

One of the quickest and best things we could do to relieve the energy shortage is to mine more surface coal. But strip mining is snarled in a maze of environmental lawsuits and legislative restraints.

Heavy social costs do, of course, result from strip mining, though the heaviest of them are light in comparison with the calamity that is building up because of the shortage of energy fuels. In recent years, environmental consciousness has induced some state legislatures to pass reclamation laws to "take the social cost out of strip mining." Some of the laws are quite severe. Coal producers must present acceptable land-reclamation plans before they can begin strip mining. If their plans are accepted, they must post land-reclamation performance bonds averaging $650 an acre.

Ben Lusk, an official of the West Virginia Surface Mining and Reclamation Association, says coal producers are now reclaiming all the land they strip, and are paying for reclamation of land stripped and abandoned years ago.

It is obvious that strip mining *changes* the land. But reclamation often makes it more productive than it was before, and also, in the eyes of some beholders, more attractive than it was. Yet nothing short of the impossible goal of restoring strip-mined land to its original condition will satisfy zealous environmentalists. The leader of the environmental zealots crusading against strip mining is Congressman Ken Hechler (D.-West Virginia). He wants a federal law to outlaw strip mining altogether, and he has tremendous support from the ecology lobby.

Congressman Hechler's bill to outlaw strip mining was given little consideration in Congress in 1972, but a bill that would have given the Secretary of the Interior power to administer a regulatory program to control such mining did pass the House. It died for lack of action by the Senate. In turning to the federal government to solve the strip-mining problem, environmentalists ignore the fact that the federal government has been a major cause of that problem.

The federal government, in trying to socialize the entire economy of the Appalachian region, has caused much despoiling of the region. When Franklin D. Roosevelt and his New Deal Congress created the Tennessee Valley Authority (TVA) in the 1930's, their promise was that TVA would bring booming prosperity to the valley of the Tennessee River.

In the name of flood control, TVA put permanently out of commission more land than was ever flooded by rivers in the Tennessee Valley, and much of it was among the richest land on this continent. On the pretext of giving the public cheap freight rates, TVA constructed an elaborate network of costly, impractical, tax-subsidized, water-transportation facilities which undercut railroad and trucking rates. This was, at first, called a by-product of flood control.

Another by-product was electrical power. The Authority was not supposed to build facilities for the sole purpose of producing power; but wherever it built a flood-control dam, it could, when practicable, make it a multipurpose dam, and produce electrical power as a by-product of flood-control activities. This would be useful, TVA proponents argued, because, by itself producing power, the government would have a yardstick to measure production costs, and it could, therefore, more equitably set and regulate rates charged by private power companies.

The yardstick became a club. Because its production was subsidized by all taxpayers, power from the TVA was sold at rates below the average charged by private industry. Far from meeting the region's needs for electrical power, TVA created a continuing power crisis. As its "cheap" prices drove private power producers out of business, private industry was denounced for failing to meet its responsibilities. So TVA began building steam-generating plants for the sole purpose of generating power, because private industry had "proven itself inadequate." Before long, TVA's principal activity was the generating of power in plants fueled with coal. It eliminated all competition from private producers of electrical power and solidified the government's socialistic monopoly on power production in the area.

As a consequence of all this, TVA is now the nation's largest producer of electrical power, and also its largest consumer of coal. Thus TVA controls the fate of the coal-bearing region, not just in the Tennessee Valley, but in the whole area known as Appalachia. And TVA sets marketing trends for coal, heavily influences technological research and development, dictates prices, and prescribes standards for industry.

In its greed for more coal to keep its power-empire going and growing, TVA for years set only one major standard for the coal industry: get the coal by whatever means possible and deliver it at the lowest possible price. It was not until 1968 that TVA began to require its coal contractors to rebuild land stripped in the mining of coal for TVA. In 1970, acknowledging that its 1968 standards were inadequate, TVA issued new standards for strip mining. But the damage had been done.

OIL REFINERIES

Conspiracy among major integrated oil firms is not a cause of gasoline scarcity in the United States. The massive increase in consumer demand, much of it caused by new government-required pollution-abatement devices on automobiles, and the failure to increase refinery capacity are the main causes of gasoline shortages.

The nation needs at least five new refineries now. According to the National Petroleum Council, 50 new refineries will be needed by 1985. Yet no refineries have been built in the eastern United States since 1969. In Maine and Delaware, state governments, influenced by the ecology lobby, have specifically prohibited refinery construction. The last refinery built anywhere in the country was completed by Mobil Oil Company at Joliet, Illinois, in 1972 — before activists could stop it with the National Environmental Policy Act.

The lead time for putting a new refinery into production (that is, the interval between decision to build and date of beginning operations) is three years at the minimum; it often runs to seven. Yet in 1973 there is still not one new refinery under construction in the United States, and none is being planned.

Although the threat of litigation by the ecology lobby has stopped the building of new refineries, the oil companies are pushing hard to expand old ones. This will ease, though it cannot solve, the refinery-shortage problem.

OIL SUPERPORTS

General George A. Lincoln (USA Retired), then director of the federal Office of Emergency Preparedness, told *U.S. News & World Report* (December 11, 1972):

"The environmental problems of where to locate new refineries and ... new superports [must] be worked out without too much further delay. If the new refineries are to operate, they must be supplied with crude oil. To deliver that crude oil ... there will have to be tankers and ports that can accommodate them. We are coming now into the age of the supertanker which, through economy of scale, cuts the cost of moving oil significantly."

A supertanker is a ship of 100,000 or more dead-weight tons. There are about 400 now in operation in the world, and an additional 300 under construction, some of them approaching 500,000 tons in size. Experts predict million-ton supertankers in the future. These supertankers require superports in deep water. Consequently, superports are often offshore, several miles out in some places. At present, there are about 150 ports in the world capable of handling the deep-draft tankers, *but not one in the United States.*

Officials of some of our maritime states have expressed unwillingness (because of the ecology lobby) to permit construction of superports on or off their shores. In the "oil states" of Texas and Louisiana there is strong support for the building of superports, but the effort is being strangled by the federal government.

In 1969, Louisiana created a special commission to study the problem of locating and building a superport. In 1972, Texas created a similar agency, called the Offshore Terminal Commission. For water deep enough (95 to 110 feet) to handle supertankers, the port must be about 30 miles offshore, well beyond the nine-mile limit of land controlled by the states. This means that federal approval must be obtained before any state can construct such a facility.

Total construction cost of a superport in the

Gulf of Mexico is estimated at $2 billion. A private corporation called Seadock, Inc., organized by 11 oil companies, plans to start construction by 1976 on a privately owned superport — if the federal government will grant permission and sell (or lease) the underwater land.

There is some possibility that the state commissions of Louisiana and Texas will cooperate with Seadock in building an offshore port; but there is controversy about it. Some want the port to be built and operated by state governments as a public utility. Others want it built by private enterprise and operated as a "common carrier" so that it can be strongly regulated by the federal government's Interstate Commerce Commission and interested state agencies.

Larry Teaver, administrative consultant for the Texas Offshore Terminal Commission, says the biggest problem in developing a superport is finding a way through the labyrinth of federal agencies claiming jurisdiction over some aspect of the operation.

OIL FROM THE ARCTIC

When Alaska became a state in 1959, the federal government transferred to state ownership several million acres of land; but about 95 percent of all land in Alaska still belongs to the federal government. Two million acres of the land given to Alaska is on the North Slope — a frozen wilderness, 1,000 miles wide, descending 150 miles northward from the Brooks Mountain Range to the Arctic Ocean.

In the 1960's, American oil firms began explorations for oil on the North Slope. In the summer of 1968, Atlantic Richfield Company, after spending $8 million, brought in two discovery wells on the tundra near Prudhoe Bay, an inlet of the Arctic Ocean near the eastern edge of the North Slope. Several firms quickly put a labor force of more than 3000 men to work drilling on three full shifts a day. They sank about 80 wells, at a cost of between $2 million and $4 million for each. The exploration activities, and the drilling to prove the field, cost the oil companies heavily; but one of the world's greatest petroleum deposits had been found — an estimated 10 billion barrels of oil and many trillions of cubic feet of natural gas.

In July 1968, Atlantic Richfield Company, Humble Oil and Refining Company, and British Petroleum Oil Corporation began preliminary studies to determine the feasibility of a pipeline to move oil from the new field. Humble also spent several million dollars to send the ice-breaker *Manhattan* on a test trip through the polar ice cap, but concluded as a result of the trip that transporting oil by tanker through the polar region to the eastern seaboard of the United States was not practicable.

Initial surveys and studies having established that pipeline transportation was feasible, a consortium of eight major oil firms (one of which later dropped out) formed the Alyeska Pipeline Service Company to engineer and build the facility. The building of the pipeline would be the largest single construction project ever undertaken by private industry. According to the plans, a 48-inch pipeline would bisect the State of Alaska, running 800 miles southward from Prudhoe Bay to ice-free water at Valdez on the Gulf of Alaska. A port with facilities to handle giant tankers would be constructed at Valdez. A fleet of tankers would be built to haul the oil from Valdez to the lower 48 states on the continent.

The pipeline would carry two million barrels of oil a day across three rugged mountain ranges, 350 streams (a few of them major rivers), and two earthquake zones. Hence, it must have built-in precautions against ruptures that might cause harm to flora or fauna. The flowing oil would be warm (up to 145 degrees), and for about 400 miles it would traverse regions where the top crust of the earth is permanently frozen. Hence, the line would be elevated or insulated (or both) to prevent melting of the permafrost.

All along the line there was a delicate ecological balance that had not yet been thoroughly investigated. Hence, in addition to engineers, geologists, and other specialists supplied by the parent oil firms, Alyeska Pipeline Service Company drew upon the resources of universities for scholars and scientific investigators to learn everything possible about the oceanography, biology, botany, zoology, ornithology, archaeology, and geology, and the engineering techniques, significant to the ecology of Alaska.

Clearing for the permanent pipeline right-of-way, access roads, and pump stations, as well as for the temporary working space needed during construction, would destroy the vegetative cover of the land in the areas involved. Hence, Alyeska specialists had to find the seeds and fertilizers best suited for fast revegetation in the hostile soil and climate.

Alyeska teams conducted a survey of fish in all 350 streams to be crossed — the first such scientific study ever made, in many instances — to make sure that neither construction activities nor permanent pipeline operations would block migration or disrupt spawning.

Specialists studied the habits of the Dall sheep, the bear, the moose, and the two great caribou herds of Alaska. In most areas where migrating herds normally cross the proposed right-of-way route, the pipeline would be buried. In the crossing areas where the 48-inch pipe had to be above ground, ramps and underpasses were to be provided for the animals. Alyeska set up a simulated pipeline with underpasses and ramps and observed the reaction of the animals, to make sure the installation did not hinder or disturb them.

Ornithologists carefully studied the route of the pipeline to make sure that none of the construction or operating activities associated with it would harm birds. Alyeska even moved one of its communication sites after discovering that it might be too close to a peregrine falcon's nest.

Archaeological teams explored along the pipeline route, making digs and recording and preserving findings at about 200 sites that might be disturbed by construction activities.

Alyeska Pipeline Service Company commissioned the Institute of Marine Science at the University of Alaska to make a biological and physical study of the harbor at Valdez to gain information needed to avoid any potential pollution problems in the Gulf of Alaska during loading of oil tankers at the pipeline terminal.

The extensive ecological research financed by Alyeska has already provided a great deal of previously unavailable information about the Alaskan wilderness, and may well result in an improvement of man's relationship with the Alaskan environment. It was a daring, thrilling, and impressive undertaking in one of the most remote regions of the earth, where nights are long and daylight hours brief for months each year, and the climate is incredibly harsh.

On September 11, 1969, the State of Alaska auctioned off to oil companies $900 million worth of oil leases.

Alyeska Pipeline Service Company then applied for permits to construct the 800-mile pipeline across the federal lands that lay in its path. The company planned to spend a billion dollars, to mobilize some 10,000 workers and assemble a colossal assortment of expensive machinery, and to start the oil flowing in three years.

But the project never got under way. It was blocked in federal courts by activist lawyers representing three small but militant environmental groups, using the National Environmental Policy Act of 1969 as their weapon.

The first assault on the pipeline, however, had been made earlier in 1969, even before the environmental law was passed. Under the legal tutelage of Ramsey Clark and Arthur Goldberg, and with the support of environmentalists generally, a small group of militant Alaskan natives filed suit to prohibit federal permits for the pipeline. The militants called themselves the Alaska Federation of Natives, and said they spoke for the 50,000 Eskimos, Indians, and Aleuts who constitute Alaska's native population. They laid claim to most of the 365-million-acre surface area of Alaska and to all minerals beneath it. Ramsey Clark and Arthur Goldberg registered as lobbyists for the militants, and testified in support of their claim.

With this preposterous claim, these imported radical lawyers blocked in federal court the granting of pipeline right-of-way permits until Congress passed the Alaska Native Claims Settlement Act. This law gave the 53,000 Alaska natives $462.5 million immediately, plus $500 million to be paid to them from state and federal mineral revenues after production in the Alaskan field begins, plus ownership title to 40 million acres of land.

Then the militant natives deserted their supporters, the militant environmentalists. With a guarantee of $500 million in revenue after the oil starts flowing, the natives want it to flow.

166

The radical environmentalists, however, have made it quite clear that they do not want an Alaska pipeline under any conditions. They do not want oil production in Alaska. Though most of them have never been in Alaska, they refer to it as "our last great wilderness." They want to keep it that way — a barren wilderness, barred from any kind of use by human beings. As Eric E. Wohlforth, revenue commissioner for the State of Alaska, puts it: "The environmentalists are trying to lock up Alaska forever."

By the time the Alaska Native Claim Settlement Act was passed (December 14, 1971), the environmentalists no longer needed their erstwhile cohorts, the Alaska Federation of Natives. The environmentalists had, and were using, the club they needed: the National Environmental Policy Act.

On April 13, 1970, six attorneys representing the Wilderness Society, Friends of the Earth, and the Environmental Defense Fund, Inc., of New York, obtained from U.S. District Court Judge George A. Hart Jr., in Washington, D.C., a preliminary injunction prohibiting the Secretary of the Interior from granting a construction permit for the Alaska pipeline. The injunction was issued on the ground that the Department of the Interior had not complied with the National Environmental Policy Act of 1969 by filing an adequate environmental-impact statement.

It took the Interior Department almost two years to prepare and file such an impact statement.

On January 24, 1972, the Annual Report of the President's Council of Economic Advisers said: "The development of the . . . [Alaskan oil] field and transportation of the oil to the West Coast would save the nation $15 billion to $17 billion during the expected 20-year life of the field."

In February 1972, the U.S. Secretary of Commerce characterized the Alaska pipeline as offering perhaps the greatest single opportunity for new cargoes and new jobs that had ever been opened to the American maritime fleet. The Secretary said: "A fleet of some 30 new supertankers would be needed to carry North Slope oil from southern Alaska to the West Coast, and constructing them would pump an estimated $1 billion through the shipbuilding industry into the economy . . . . When the minimized [environmental] risks are weighed against the great need for the pipeline and its potential benefits, I am certain that it must be built."

Finally, on March 20, 1972, the Interior Department released a six-volume study, called *Final Environmental Statement on the Proposed Trans Alaska Pipeline*, accompanied by a three-volume analysis of economic and national-security reasons for building the pipeline. Among the national-security reasons specified was the need to reduce our dependence on foreign sources of oil. The impact statement and the analysis concluded that overriding national interests made construction of the Alaska pipeline desirable, even though some environmental risk was involved.

However, regardless of the overriding national interests, the Secretary of the Interior could not issue permits for the pipeline immediately. Under the incredible environmental law, the environmentalists had 45 days to file comments on the impact statement. On May 11, 1972, at the expiration of the 45-day period, the Secretary of the Interior announced that he would issue permits for construction of the Alaska pipeline. But, again, he could not issue the permits immediately. Under court orders, he had to wait at least two weeks to give environmentalists time to prepare their legal response.

Three months went by, while the environmentalists prepared, filed, and argued their response. They finally lost in U.S. District Court. On August 17, 1972, Judge George L. Hart lifted his injunction, which for 28 months had blocked permits to construct the Alaska pipeline. One week later, the environmentalists appealed to the U.S. Court of Appeals in the District of Columbia.

There a startling thing happened. The environmental groups had legal standing to attack the Alaska pipeline only under the National Environmental Policy Act, and only on environmental grounds. All of their legal action in the case was on that basis, including their August 22, 1972 appeal. Up to that time, environment had been the sole issue in the case. When the appellate court handed down its decision on

February 21, 1973, however, the court did not deal with the environmental issue or with the National Environmental Policy Act under which the case had been brought. The appellate court held that the Secretary of the Interior cannot grant a right-of-way across Alaska unless Congress amends the Mineral Lands Leasing Act of 1920, because this law, the court said, limits right-of-way grants to narrower widths than that planned for the Alaskan pipeline.

On February 21, 1973, the two U.S. Senators from Alaska introduced a bill to divest federal courts of jurisdiction over the Alaska pipeline.

On February 27, 1973, the Secretary of the Interior said the administration would ask Congress to amend the Mineral Lands Leasing Act of 1920. No such bill was reported in the Senate until July, or in the House until August. The Secretary of the Interior also said he would appeal the appellate court decision. Government lawyers handling the case, however, said they did not have as good a case for appeal as they would have had if the appellate court decision had been based on environmental grounds.

As this is being written (August 1973), the Congress has just revised the Mineral Lands Leasing Act of 1920 to permit construction on the pipeline to begin. But, of course, the environmentalists are preparing more lawsuits.

For more than four years, productive activity at Prudhoe Bay has been stopped. The oil companies have sustained a payroll for about 300 men who remain in otherwise-deserted camps to guard mountains of pipes and fleets of idle bulldozers, trucks, and other machinery. More than a billion dollars of private capital has also been tied up and idled; and the nation has been denied two million barrels of oil a day that could already be flowing through the pipeline.

In the summer of 1973, in the midst of a serious fuel shortage, Senator Henry Jackson, chief architect of the National Environmental Policy Act, which stopped the Alaska pipeline, said: "I think it's outrageous we can't import oil from Alaska."

OIL FROM THE SEAS

Speaking in May, 1972, G.J. Tankersley, president of East Ohio Gas Company, warned: "At a time of desperate energy crisis, a major sale of offshore oil and gas leases has been delayed . . . by a small group of well-meaning conservationists who, relying on sections of the new Environmental Protection Act, are exercising the power to assure that some citizens will be cold and dark at some future date. The last offshore lease sale returned $845 million to the U.S. Treasury. But by posting a hundred-dollar bond, these conservationists, expressing concern for possible pollution of off-shore waters, have been able to thwart the quest for desperately needed clean energy supplies . . . ."

This was, of course, a part of the cost of the 600 Santa Barbara birds involved in the 1969 oil spill. And the situation has not improved since Mr. Tankersley mentioned it in 1972. It is quite a story, deserving more filling in with background and detail.

By the mid-1950's, most oil that was relatively easy to find and produce within the United States had already been discovered and tapped. From then on, exploration became increasingly more expensive. New discoveries were in more remote, inaccessible areas. Wells had to be sunk to greater, costlier depths. This natural escalation of costs was accelerated by the federal government's reckless, irresponsible domestic spending and foreign giveaways, which inflated our currency and multiplied the price of everything.

It can now cost as much as $5 million to drill one deep oil well within the United States. The average cost of all wells today is about $100,000 per well, in contrast with $55,000 as recently as 1960. These are costs of drilling on land. Drilling in the ocean is more expensive.

Oil companies began seriously searching the oceans for new sources of supply in the late 1940's. They found that the potential for offshore production is almost limitless. Under the outer continental shelf along the east coast, in the Gulf of Mexico, in the Santa Barbara Channel, and in the Gulf of Alaska there is now known to be enough oil and natural gas to last this nation for centuries — if all of it could be produced.

The first well drilled out of sight of land was completed in 1947. In 1953, Congress enacted the Outer Continental Shelf Lands Act, establishing federal control of oil and gas resources on offshore lands extending outward underwater from U.S. shorelines — as far as 150 miles in some areas. The act authorized the Interior Department to sell leases on a competitive-bid system for oil and gas extraction, with lease proceeds and subsequent royalties to go into the general revenue fund of the U.S. Treasury.

There are now about 14,000 wells in United States waters, producing 1.5 million barrels of oil daily. The invested private capital totals billions of dollars. The investment is so great, in fact, that according to Dr. Thomas D. Barrow, president of Humble Oil and Refining Company, the oil industry has not yet reached the point of making a net profit from offshore operations. Dr. Barrow estimates, however, that by the end of 1970 state and local governments had realized from offshore oil operations net revenues, in bonuses, leases, and royalties paid by oil companies, totaling about $6 billion.

This does not mean, or imply, that oil companies are engaged in offshore activities for humanitarian or public-service reasons. No oil firm or any other business whose management has good sense will go voluntarily into a costly enterprise that offers no prospect of reasonable profit; but wherever there is reasonable prospect of profit, oil companies, big and small, are always in a competitive scramble to move their equipment in and get started, even when they have to pool resources to meet the monumental costs common to all in the development of a new field. There is a bright prospect in offshore oil. If government will remove its unnecessary road blocks and get out of the way, huge capital investments in offshore facilities can be amortized and good profits can ultimately be made, despite extremely heavy costs.

At present, just a drilling platform, adequate for operations at the relatively shallow depth of 150 feet in the relatively calm waters of the Gulf of Mexico, costs about $2 million. For a depth of 400 feet, a platform costs $6 million; and the cost is $32 million for drilling in 800 feet of water. Oil companies have developed semi-submersible rigs capable of drilling beneath water 1000 feet deep. It is estimated that drilling in waters of such depth, where waves can be 100 feet high, could run the development cost of a new field to more than a billion dollars.

Oil companies are eager to undertake such ventures, but the federal government will not permit them to do so. Practically all offshore oil wells in U.S. waters are in the Gulf of Mexico and the Santa Barbara Channel. No well has ever been drilled in the area of greatest potential — the outer continental shelf along the east coast — because the federal government has never sold a lease there. This is one of the significant consequences of the Santa Barbara oil spill of 1969 and of the National Environmental Policy Act, which was an outgrowth of that accident. It is interesting in this connection to note the testimony of John M. Houchin, deputy chairman of Phillips Petroleum Company, before the

Senate Interior and Insular Affairs Committee in April of 1972. Mr. Houchin said that, of the 14,000 wells drilled in United States waters during 20 years of offshore operations, only 25 had ever had blowouts that caused a pollution problem; of the 25, only three resulted in major oil spills; and of those three major spills, none caused any lasting harm to the environment.

In his first energy message to the Congress (June 4, 1971), President Nixon said, concerning offshore production of oil and gas:

> Our ability to tap the great potential of offshore areas has been seriously hampered by . . . environmental problems.
>
> The Department of the Interior has significantly strengthened the environmental protection requirements controlling offshore drilling and we will continue to enforce these requirements very strictly. As a prerequisite to Federal lease sales, environmental assessments will be made in accordance with Section 102 of the National Environmental Policy Act of 1969 . . . .
>
> In order to expand productive possibilities as rapidly as possible, the accelerated program should include the sale of new leases not only in the highly productive Gulf of Mexico, but also in some other promising areas. I am therefore directing the Secretary of the Interior to increase the offerings of oil and gas leases and to publish a schedule for lease offerings on the Outer Continental Shelf during the next five years, beginning with a general lease sale . . . this year.

Immediately following that Presidential message, the Interior Secretary scheduled sales of major offshore oil and gas leases for each year through 1975. The leases were to be offered chiefly in the Gulf of Mexico; but some were to be sold in the Gulf of Alaska, and some (for the first time ever) on the Atlantic outer continental shelf.

In November 1971, a group of 60 Congressmen from eastern states demanded that the Interior Department cancel its planned sale of leases off the Atlantic coast.

The Interior Department scheduled a date in December 1971 for the sale of leases in the Gulf of Mexico. Three weeks before the scheduled date, an environmental group (Natural Resources Defense Council) filed suit in U.S. District Court in Washington, D.C., contending that the Department had failed to prepare an adequate environmental-impact statement, as required by the National Environmental Policy Act of 1969. The federal judge upheld the contention, and forbade the leasing of 366,000 acres off the coast of Louisiana. Early in 1972, a U.S. Court of Appeals upheld the lower court.

It took the Interior Department several months to prepare the impact statement the courts required. The Department was not prepared to offer any more offshore leases until late 1972, when it auctioned off to private oil companies 178 tracts in the Gulf of Mexico. Net revenue to the federal government from these sales was $2.2 billion, plus continuing royalties on whatever production may eventually result from the leases.

The government's leasing program in the Gulf of Mexico, where leasing and drilling had been going on for almost 20 years, had thus been interrupted for a year. Leasing off the Atlantic coast, where there is an estimated 42 billion barrels of oil and 228 trillion cubic feet of natural gas, was stopped completely, and as of mid-1973, the government has not even sold leases for exploration there.

NATURAL GAS AND FINALE

For several years, natural gas was a nuisance to oil producers. Whenever found (usually by accident) in wells drilled for oil, gas was flared (burned off at the wellhead) to keep it from polluting the air, because there was nothing else to do with it. When adequate technology for refining, transporting, and using natural gas was developed, it became the most popular of fuels. It also became a boon to oil producers by helping to pay for the costly and hazardous activity of finding and drilling new wells.

The Natural Gas Act of 1938 gave the Federal Power Commission (FPC) regulatory authority over transportation and distribution of gas in interstate commerce. But Section 1 (b) of the Act says: "The provisions of this Act . . . shall not apply . . . to the production or gathering of natural gas." Why did Congress exempt production of natural gas from federal controls, while imposing controls on transportation and distribution?

Transporters of natural gas in interstate commerce are pipeline companies. They are generally given a monopoly (by the federal government) to serve distributing companies in certain areas. Distributors of natural gas are firms that sell it to consumers. Government at one level or another (usually local) gives the distributor a monopoly to sell gas in a certain city or metropolitan community. Hence, transporters and distributors of natural gas are, in essence, public utilities. Government shelters them from competition, guarantees them a "fair" profit, grants them special powers (right of eminent domain, for example), and therefore regulates them.

Since transporters and distributors of natural gas operate in a government-protected market, government regulation is at least possible. Their costs are measurable. The capital investment necessary to lay a pipeline or build a distributing system in a city can be rather well calculated in advance, and so can the costs of depreciation, replacement, operation, expansion, dividends to stockholders, and interest payments to lenders. Taking all of these determinable elements into account, government regulators can do a "fair" job of setting prices for the transportation and distribution of natural gas.

None of this applies, however, to the *producer* of natural gas. His costs are immeasurable. There is no way to calculate in advance the cost of finding and drilling a well. The entire industry's long-range average of eight dry holes for every one producing well is no guide for individual cases. One operator might drill 20 dry holes before hitting. Another, luckier operator might drill ten good wells in a row. Moreover, one well that costs a great deal to drill might yield a very low return, while a well that costs much less might yield a high return. It is impossible for a regulatory agency to know how much should be charged for the production of natural gas.

Only the unrestricted force of competition in a free market where the customer is king can equitably determine how much the customer should pay for natural gas at the wellhead. And production of natural gas is very competitive. Since a producer receives no monopolistic grant of sheltered markets, guaranteed profit, or any other special privilege from government, he must compete vigorously for profits from satisfied customers, to offset the immense risks and high costs which he and his financial backers carry without any guarantees from government.

After World War II, the natural gas business boomed. Before long, there were more miles of pipelines than of railroads in the United States, transporting gas to distributors all over the country. Although there were literally thousands of producers in widely scattered gas fields, most production was in five states: Texas, Louisiana, Oklahoma, New Mexico, and Kansas. Politicians in non-producing areas — especially in northern and northeastern states — initiated and never stopped a barrage of vote-getting propaganda against the "super-rich" oil men of the southwest, claiming they were abusing their "monopoly" of natural gas production by overcharging consumers, who were at their mercy. They demanded that the Federal Power Commission (FPC) protect consumers by regulating the price of natural gas at the wellhead.

In ten different cases brought before it by 1950, the FPC ruled that it had no authority to regulate wellhead sales of natural gas by independent producers and gatherers.

In truth, the cost of natural gas to the consumer was less than that of competing fuels. And most of what the consumer paid for natural gas did not go to the unregulated, competitive producers; it went to the regulated, monopolistic transporters and distributors. Of every dollar paid for gas by consumers in the north and northeast, more than 90 cents went to transporters and distributors; less than ten cents went to producers.

But the truth did not in the end prevail. The Phillips Petroleum Case, in which lies triumphed over truth, was a critical turning point in the history not only of the oil industry but of the United States — of the world, really. Phillips, an independent company, produced, gathered, and processed — in the state of Oklahoma — natural gas which it sold, in Oklahoma, to five pipeline companies. The pipeline companies transported the gas and sold it in 14 different states. In 1951, an agency of the state of Wisconsin asked the FPC to determine whether Phillips was charging reasonable prices for gas ultimately delivered to consumers in Wisconsin. (At that time, only six cents of every dollar paid by natural gas consumers in Madison, Wisconsin, went to the unregulated producer; the remaining 94 cents went to the regulated transporter and distributor). For the eleventh time, the FPC ruled that it had no jurisdiction for such regulation.

Wisconsin appealed to the federal courts. On June 7, 1954, the Supreme Court (in a 5-3 decision) decided that the Natural Gas Act of 1938, despite the language of the statute and the clear intent of the Congress that passed it, gave the FPC regulatory authority over the production of natural gas in such situations as the one at hand. The court ordered the FPC to exercise that authority.

The Federal Power Commission quickly complied. It issued orders going far beyond mere price control. Under FPC rules, a gas producer cannot make a valid contract with customers. Any contract a producer makes can be arbitrarily changed, immediately or years later, by the FPC. If the change involves reducing price below what the contract called for, the producer must make rebates. If the contract calls for the delivery of a certain quantity of gas over a certain period of time, the FPC can order the producer to deliver more, or less, than the contract stipulates; and at the end of the contract period, the producer may not terminate deliveries unless and until the FPC gives him specific permission to do so.

When strident political demands for government regulation of natural gas production began, before 1954, free-market economists and Constitutional conservatives as well as spokesmen for the oil and gas industry warned against regulation and predicted what would happen:

● Government would burden the industry with costly delays and paperwork; would create hazardous uncertainty about the validity of contracts between producers and their customers; would impose rigid, unreasonably low prices unrelated to the law of supply and demand in a competitive market, and not reflecting the declining value of government-inflated money.

● Domestic development of new sources of petroleum would decline, while demand would continue to grow. The eventual result would be a fuel shortage which, in turn, would produce shortages in all other goods and services.

● Big, integrated firms (those which not only produce petroleum but also own or control the transportation and distribution facilities) could survive, and even thrive, by going into conglomerate activities and turning away from domestic production in favor of foreign production. But independent producers would gradually vanish. As they lost investors seeking more promising places to put their money, the independent producers would also lose their key personnel, who would be seeking more promising places to invest their talents, training, and time. Step by step, the know-how and financial base for an important segment of domestic petroleum exploration in the United States would thus be dismantled.

These warnings, made in the 1950's, were ignored; but the predictions made then are now proving accurate.

Between 1950 and 1970, the U.S. consumer price index rose 61 percent; the cost of all services rose 107 percent; the cost of coal rose 80 percent; the cost of gas-well development rose more than 60 percent; the cost of gas-well maintenance and operation rose more than 80 percent; but the FPC had allowed the price of natural gas to rise only 20 percent.

By 1970, the number of new wells drilled annually in the United States had dropped to one-third of the number being drilled annually in 1954, when the government first stepped in with regulations to "insure a continued supply of low cost energy."

Those who demanded federal controls of natural gas prices at the wellhead in 1954 said that controls were necessary to prevent large producers from getting a near monopoly. At that time, the ten largest companies were producing less than one-third of the gas used in this country. Now, 19 years after controls were imposed, six large companies produce more than half of all gas produced in the United States.

In 1972, new customers in almost half the states of the union were unable to get any natural gas at all; and existing customers in many cities were experiencing shortages. At the same time, 272 million cubic feet of natural gas found in oil wells in the Gulf of Mexico was being flared every day. That is enough gas to serve a city with a population of one million. Because of the low prices fixed by FPC, however, the oil companies could not afford to build pipelines and other facilities needed to transport the gas to onshore pipelines for distribution to consumers.

In 1972, when the government-fixed wellhead price of domestically produced natural gas was 26 cents per 1000 cubic feet, American firms (with the blessing of government) contracted to import from Communist Algeria liquefied natural gas whose starting price into U.S. pipelines was to be one dollar per 1000 cubic feet. United States firms (also with the blessing of government) were talking seriously with Soviet officials about importing liquefied natural gas from Siberia. The starting price of this gas into U.S. pipelines will be considerably above one dollar per 1000 cubic feet. If this Soviet deal goes through, the United States Government will have to invest about $6 billion in Siberian facilities to liquefy the gas, before it can be shipped to the United States. Many politicians and consumer advocates, who denounce the American oil and gas industry for gouging the public, express satisfaction with the prospect of American taxpayers' first financing liquefaction facilities in the Soviet Union and then paying some four times as much for the Soviet gas as for American-produced gas.

In mid-1973, Senator Hubert Humphrey (D.-Minn.) was saying that grain farmers, processors, and haulers in the upper Midwest were uncertain whether they could get enough oil and gas to harvest their 1973 grain crops, cure them (with heaters fired by natural gas), and transport them to market. If the oil and gas shortage became that bad, Senator Humphrey predicted, there would ensue a worldwide famine the like of which the world had never seen. Senator Humphrey laid it on a bit thick, perhaps, because he wants more punitive government action against the petroleum industry. He does not appear to realize that the situation he now deplores was produced by the policies he has himself advocated for more than a quarter of a century.

The decline in U.S. domestic oil and gas exploration was rather steady from 1954 through 1969, and has accelerated somewhat since 1969. The Tax Reform Act of 1969 reduced the depletion allowance to producers on petroleum products from 27.5 percent to 22 percent, thus further decreasing the incentive for investors to put their money into oil exploration. Senator John Tower (R.-Texas) says the 1969 tax change cost the petroleum industry between $500 million and $700 million in revenue each year.

"Depletion allowance" is generally used like an expletive of hate by baiters of the petroleum industry. There have been very few "Liberal" Members of Congress elected since World War II who have not at some time publicly denounced depletion allowances as government's gift of the poor man's tax money to the super-rich oil barons. Pragmatically, a case for depletion allowance can be made on grounds that the petroleum industry is unique; that risks are abnormally great and costs immeasurable; and that the capital resource purchased by so much cost and risk is used up in the production, unlike the capital resource of a factory, which, if kept in repair, can continue to produce indefinitely.

Idealistically, there is no defense for depletion allowance. When taxes are designed to provide incentives for one activity and discourage or prohibit another; to allow this, or disallow that; to show special concern for special classes of citizens — then the taxing system is inherently corrupt and inequitable. Such a taxing system inevitably distorts and damages the economy; and it always debauches vast numbers of taxpayers by making tax cheaters of them; intimidating them into silent toleration of harmful government activities; inducing them to support politicians and political proposals they know to be bad because the support brings them promise of special favors.

That is the kind of federal taxing system the United States has. Federal tax codes discriminate against the prosperous and in favor of the poor, by imposing a progressively higher percentage tax on the prosperous. They discriminate against the poor and the wage earner and in favor of the rich, by making it possible for high-income individuals to get exemptions, write-offs, and credits not available to low-income taxpayers and wage earners. And they discriminate against all taxpayers and in favor of rich, powerful lobbyists for confiscatory taxation by giving the lobbyists (that is, unions, foundations, consumer advocate groups, church organizations, and so on) total exemption from the taxation they want imposed on everyone else.

The system cannot be reformed. It must be abolished and replaced by an equitable system designed for the exclusive purpose of raising needed revenue. In such a system, individuals would all be taxed indiscriminately on the same basis, with politicians and government officials allowed absolutely no opportunity to grant special exemptions, privileges, allowances, or benefactions of any kind to anyone. Until this is accomplished, however, we had better have (and soon) enough depletion allowance for the petroleum industry to encourage vast investment of private capital in domestic exploration for new sources of energy.

A series of events in 1972 and 1973 may serve to indicate how the American petroleum industry is whipsawed by government policies and lobbyists to whom government gives tax exemption.

Early in 1972, there was talk in Administration circles in Washington that President Nixon might suggest decontrolling gas prices for all production from new wells as one means of encouraging more exploration. Forces mobilized to resist such decontrol.

Two mild-mannered bills were introduced in the Senate in 1972 – not to decontrol natural gas, but to guarantee the sanctity of contracts so that natural-gas producers may know what price they may receive for their product and the amount of gas they must deliver on a particular contract. Even this much "concession" to the industry was too much. David W. Calfee, an attorney from Ralph Nader's Public Interest Groups, testified against the sanctity-of-contract bills, saying they were "an attempt to achieve indirectly the decontrol of natural gas prices." Although the chairman of the Federal Power Commission testified in favor of them, neither bill even got out of committee.

By December 1972, organized environmentalists, who with government help have done the most in the past four years to create an energy crisis, were leading a kind of national chorus of defamation against the petroleum industry for creating the crisis. They blamed the industry specifically for the very deficiencies the environmentalists themselves were responsible for: not producing enough oil and gas and not building new refineries. They accused the oil companies of monopolistic practices, of deliberately withholding reserves, and of price juggling.

On March 6, 1973, President Nixon reimposed restraints on most of the oil industry, limiting price increases for crude oil and most petroleum products to 1.0 or 1.5 percent. This was the first sign of "tightening-up to control inflation" under Phase III of the President's price-control program. It seemed unusually stiff, because prices in general were rising much faster than that, and wages were soaring.

On April 18, 1973, in the second "energy message" he had sent to the Congress in less than two years, the President suggested stimulating petroleum production by easing up on the industry a bit. His main action, however, discouraged domestic production. The President used his Executive power to remove all tariffs and quotas on imports of foreign oil and to institute a complicated scaled system of license fees (which amount to a very low per-barrel tariff) to regulate imports of foreign oil. To stimulate construction of refineries, the President suggested that all new refineries be exempt from paying any fees on imported crude oil for five years after construction. And to stimulate exploration for natural gas, the President made the proposal which had been rumored for more than a year: that gas produced from new wells be decontrolled.

A few days after this message was delivered, one of the top leaders of the nationally organized, tax-exempt lobby against the petroleum industry addressed the National Press Club in Washington. The speaker was Lee C. White, representing Consumers Federation of America, an amalgam of 14 consumerist groups. Mr. White was formerly chairman of the Federal Power Commission.

White said he favored formation of government companies in the fuels industry, particularly for the development of resources on public lands. The primary purpose of this, he said, would be to provide a cost yardstick so that the government and the public would know the true cost of producing energy. He also asserted that government companies would be more likely to protect the environment and the public than profit-motivated industry would be.

In the last week of May 1973, the Federal Power Commission, on the basis of industry claims that proven reserves of natural gas were growing critically short, granted producers a significant increase in the price of gas from any new wells brought in. One week later, the antitrust division of the Department of Justice filed court action against nine major oil firms intended to force them to give documented proof of the actual existence of the shortage they alleged.

On June 5, 1973, Senators Henry M. Jackson and James Abourezk (D.-South Dakota), supported by several other Members of both Houses of Congress, stated that the current gasoline shortages "seem to be a contrivance of the major oil companies." They demanded a federal investigation.

In the last week of June 1973, Senator Philip Hart (D.-Michigan), one of the foremost foes of the oil industry, held a public hearing before his Antitrust Subcommittee to investigate the fuel shortage. Most of the witnesses shared Hart's view that the industry was responsible for it.

David Schwartz, assistant chief of the FPC

office of economics, said that the higher prices which the FPC had recently granted gas producers were causing supply shortages. Schwartz said producers were keeping gas in the ground to force FPC to grant even higher prices. (This allegation was belied by the facts: because of price increases and the remote hope for decontrol of new wells, the number of new gas-producing wells brought in during the first six months of 1973 exceeded by 53 percent the number brought in during the same period in 1972.) One U.S. Representative told the Hart Subcommittee that federal regulation of natural-gas production should be *extended* to intrastate sales. Several witnesses repeated the suggestion made to the Press Club a few weeks before by the Consumers Federation of America, namely, that government companies be established to develop and produce oil and gas resources on public lands and offshore. And there was support for a bill introduced by Senator Thomas Eagleton (D.-Missouri), to break up the big integrated oil companies — require them to sell their service stations and stop retailing gasoline and other petroleum products.

The Eagleton bill had the support of many independent service-station operators. Congress has no constitutional authority, of course, to enact such legislation. If enacted, it will do great harm, and no good. Bigness does not mean monopoly. Generally, the bigger companies get, the fiercer is the competition among them; and the fiercer the competition is, the more the public benefits. If subjected to this kind of pressure from market competition, but left free from harassing government controls and punitive taxation, the big oil companies could produce more petroleum products for sale at lower prices. Far from being hurt, independent service stations would benefit, along with the general public. In a wide-open free market, there would be plenty of non-integrated producers bidding for the wholesale business of independent distributors.

Our country desperately needs the big combines of private wealth represented by the oil industry majors. It has already taken billions of dollars to explore and prove the Alaskan North Slope oil field. It will take billions more to build the pipeline, to build a fleet of supertankers, and to build ports to handle the tankers. It takes billions to discover and develop major offshore oil fields. Only through bigness of business can such amounts of private capital be raised. Without it, our economy will stagnate and degenerate — either through cessation of further effort to develop our fuel resources, or through the turning over of the effort to government. Either way, our economy will be doomed.

One notable remark of 1973 needs further comment. It is the suggestion of Lee C. White of the Consumers Federation of America that government companies producing energy fuels would protect the environment better than profit-motivated private companies would. The record proves the exact opposite.

As was noted in an earlier chapter, of the four

pollution cases serious enough to reach the U.S. Supreme Court during the first 182 years of our history, three were against various levels of government.

There has been much doomsday talk about pollution of the Great Lakes. Lake Erie, we were told, was a dead lake, so polluted that commercial fishing was no longer allowed. Other lakes were dying, and all were menaced by pollution. For the most part, we were led to believe that private industry was the main villain. As it turns out, the reports were exaggerated. The 1971 fish catch in Lake Erie was the biggest ever recorded. Lake Michigan was not nearly as foul as earlier hysteria had indicated; and the other Great Lakes were in rather good condition. To be sure, Erie and Michigan are polluted; and the other magnificent bodies of water suffer some contamination. But who has done most of the polluting? Governments.

In his April 15, 1970, message to Congress on pollution of the Great Lakes, President Nixon specifically named the Army Corps of Engineers as a prime polluter of the lakes. He asked Congress to outlaw dumping of contaminated dredge spoil from federal projects. Who else pollutes the lakes? Primarily, some 100 or more city governments, dumping improperly treated sewage. We should also remember TVA's contribution to strip-mining pollution in Appalachia.

The main argument offered for establishing government fuel-producing companies probably needs no comment, but it is difficult to refrain from making one. We are told that government production would be a yardstick for measuring the true cost of production, and so on. It is the old TVA argument of the 1930's all over again, almost word for word, and the people making it now have the same objectives as those who made it then. They are out to harass private industry until it cannot function properly, to condemn it for improper functioning, and then to drive it out of existence.

This is the way its foes intend to administer the *coup de grâce* that will kill the fuel-energy business – and the American way of life.

Chapter Twelve

Cleaning Up
And Trussing Up

FROM 1952 to 1969, the federal government invested about $15 billion in building 7500 municipal sewage treatment plants and other water treatment facilities. And in November of 1969, David D. Dominick, commissioner of the Federal Water Pollution Control Administration, said: "In the last 10 years, the quality of the nation's water has probably degenerated."

So Congress enacted the Water Quality Improvement Act of 1970. That did not do enough good; so President Nixon asked Congress to pass another pure-water bill. Meanwhile, the President dug up an old law which had been on the statute books unenforced for 71 years — the Rivers and Harbors Act of 1899 — and used it as the basis for an Executive Order issued December 12, 1970, requiring industries to obtain federal permits before discharging waste materials into navigable waters.

Congress complied with the President's request for a new water bill by passing the Clean-Water Act of 1972, authorizing $24.7 billion in federal expenditures. This was more than the President wanted. He called it inflation-ary, and vetoed it. Congress passed it over his veto.

President Nixon complained about the heavy tax cost of the Clean-Water Act, but the corollary costs will be even heavier. The corollary costs are those imposed on 250,000 water-using factories to meet requirements of the Act. Many factories have already been shut down because of the law. It is estimated that when the clean-water program is in full operation and all its corollary costs are passed on to consumers, as they must be, the total cost to all consumers in the nation will be above $30 billion a year — $480 a year for every American family.

The consumer advocate's consummate skill in transforming governmental failure into an excuse for more of the same is matched by his acumen in fastening upon a legitimate public problem and making it worse by sensational allegations and unreasonable demands for an instant solution. The furor about automobile safety and automobile pollution illustrates the point.

With all its deficiencies and its enormous complexities, with which only highly trained mechanics can hope to cope when anything goes wrong, the modern automobile is still a miraculous product. The average new car is made up of about 15,000 parts. Each part has an average of about 100 characteristics. This means that the number of defects possible in every new car is about 1.5 million.

This complex machine is mass-produced under government-imposed conditions that make the goal of perfection unattainable. Federal laws deny management the right to select, discipline, and control its own labor force. Federal "Civil Rights" laws force management to hire incompetent, indifferent, untrained people, many of whom never become reliable workmen. Worst of all, federal labor laws give monopolistic control over the labor force to unions. Unions, which are not held accountable for shoddy workmanship, often cause it by the attitudes they inculcate in workmen and by the work rules they impose. Unions will not permit management (which *is* held accountable for poor workmanship) to reward reliable workers or to fire or otherwise discipline the unreliable.

In view of these facts about the complexity of modern cars and about the government-imposed conditions under which they are manufactured, it is a wonder that such mass-produced machines, operated by millions of individuals who know little or nothing about proper care and maintenance, can function at all. Yet, thanks to expensively elaborate inspecting and testing procedures established by management, the average new car produced in the United States has a 99.95 percent probability of starting and operating properly on demand — a higher percentage of reliability than exists in some parts of the equipment used in Apollo spaceflight missions.

Obviously, putting the major blame for automobile accidents on automobile manufacturers (as consumer advocates do) gets the problem out of focus, and produces remedies which harm rather than help the consumer. Consumers have already been forced to buy an assortment of safety devices which most of them refused to buy when they had a free choice; and in the future they will be compelled to buy devices even more expensive and cumbersome than those of the present. But all the safety devices that can be imagined by consumer advocates and produced by automotive engineers will give consumers little protection against cars careening along public thoroughfares with drunks behind the wheel. Faulty operators — people — are responsible for almost all of the carnage which consumer advocates blame on the business organizations that produce cars.

On 1973-model cars, consumers are already paying from $30 to $50 for a lap belt equipped with light and buzzer which are activated if the belt is not fastened. Many motorists disconnect the device or deactivate it by buckling it behind them. Since some consumers will not use this expensive device that government forces them to buy, government has decided to protect them by making all consumers purchase a more expensive device which they will be forced to use, and which will probably impair the operating efficiency of their cars.

On April 19, 1973, the National Highway Traffic Safety Administration announced that it would require an "interlock system" on all cars manufactured after August 15, 1973. With this system installed in a car, driver and front-seat passenger must have combination lap-and-shoulder-belts fastened around them before the car can be started. Deactivating this new rig so that the car can operate without it will necessitate major changes by a skilled mechanic. Car industry officials warn that the new device will be very costly, will make cars difficult to start, and may, because of its complexity, have a malfunction rate as high as 3 percent during the first year of operation.

In response to these warnings from industry, the National Highway Traffic Safety Administration amended its interlock system requirement to include an alternative system — which will allow a car engine to be started but prevent the vehicle from *moving* until driver and front-seat passenger are fully trussed up in the federally required harness. But other devices aimed at pollution abatement that government will force consumers to buy may add more hazards to car driving than government-required safety equipment can eliminate. The price to consumers of thus making matters worse for them will be very high.

Some pollution-abatement devices on cars are desirable. But with only the conventional devices that industry has been putting on cars for years, automobile pollution would be reduced substantially by proper maintenance and operation of individual cars. Alexander Rihm Jr., director of the Air Pollution Control Program of the New York State Department of Environmental Conservation, says: "One dead sparkplug in a car can increase the pollutant emissions by 10 to 15 times. One sparkplug misfiring may double the output of hydrocarbons. A carburetor set too rich can increase carbon monoxide by 50 percent or more. We might do more by worrying less about ... emission control devices and worrying more about maintaining our individual vehicles."

But consumer misuse of automobiles as a cause of pollution has been ignored by consumer advocates. They direct their attack on business for producing the machines. Indeed, some (Environmental Action, for example) want Congress to limit car production. Others (Representative Leonard Farbstein, D.-New York, for example) want Congress to outlaw the internal-combustion engine.

In the early 1960's, before consumer advocates seized upon automobile pollution as a cause to serve their own ends, automobile manufacturers responded to growing public concern by intensifying research programs to develop means of reducing noxious emissions from gasoline motors. By the time 1968 models went into production, the manufacturers had developed and installed devices which reduced harmful emissions significantly. Newer devices for models to be produced after 1968 were being tested. Automobile manufacturers seemed to be making orderly progress; but organized consumerism stopped orderly progression.

Responding to consumerist pressures, President Nixon helped push through the House of Representatives the Clean-Air Amendments Act of 1970. As passed by the House, the Act directed the Environmental Protection Agency to tighten restrictions and speed progress toward almost-total elimination of objectionable automobile emissions. The EPA announced that, under terms of the House-passed bill, it would propose for 1975 models elimination of 85 percent or more of undesirable emissions, and would set 1980 as a target year for eliminating more than 90 percent of all such emissions. The EPA acknowledged that a technological breakthrough would be necessary to meet this goal, and indicated that the goal would not be set as an inflexible deadline if the breakthrough did not occur.

When the House-passed Clean-Air Amendments Act of 1970 reached the Senate Subcommittee on Air and Water Pollution, Senator Edmund Muskie (D.-Maine), the chairman, decided, as he expressed it, "to put the auto companies' feet to the fire." Ignoring technological problems and ultimate cost to consumers, Muskie inserted a provision establishing a rigid deadline of 1975-76 for meeting the emission-control standards for new cars. When automotive engineers explained the technological impossibility of meeting such requirements in a year and a half, Muskie dismissed them, saying he was leaving it up to their ingenuity to produce these results.

Other Senators on the Subcommittee perceived that if the automotive engineers were right and Muskie wrong about the technological feasibility of meeting Muskie's deadline, the bill would cause economic catastrophe – that is, sudden, total shutdown of America's leading industry. They suggested a provision in the Clean-Air Amendments Act requiring a finding by an impartial committee of the National Academy of Sciences. If such a committee found that automobile manufacturers had made all possible efforts to meet the deadline for 1975-1976 models, the EPA administrator could give them a one-year extension.

Muskie, after being outvoted 10 to 3, agreed to accept this concession if his colleagues would accept another requirement. He wanted to require manufacturers to guarantee that each new car would maintain its original low emission level for 50,000 miles or five years. With this Muskie provision added, the Clean-Air Amendments Act of 1970 went to the Senate for a vote. It passed, 73 to 0; the House acquiesced; and President Nixon signed the bill into law on December 31, 1970. The Presidential signing of the Clean-Air Amendments Act on the last day of the year, with the press and select Members of Congress invited, was another theatrical production of the kind that had been staged to launch the National Environmental Policy Act on the first day of the same year – but with one political overtone added: though the clean-air law was known as the Muskie Bill, Senator Muskie was not invited to the White House ceremony.

The Clean-Air Amendments Act of 1970 authorized expenditures of $1.1 billion for fiscal years 1971-1973. This huge cost would be borne, of course, by the consumers to be protected. Other big new costs were also piled up for consumers to pay. When the Act became law, the Ford Motor Company increased its budget for emission-control research from $65 million in 1970 to $132 million in 1971; General Motors Corporation, from $150 million in 1971 to $225 million in 1972. Chrysler and American Motors made proportionate increases. All told, the four automobile companies put some 8000 engineers and technicians to work full-time to meet the government's schedule for production of required emission-control devices.

Something resembling a Rube Goldberg fantasy resulted. A device which decreased one kind of harmful emission would increase another kind. This required another device, which in turn required another. One complicated gadget developed in the process is called a catalytic converter. Industry fears that it may not be effective or durable in actual consumer use, but it represents industry's only chance of meeting the extreme standards and early deadlines set by the EPA.

While manufacturers were working to comply with the Clean-Air Amendments Act of 1970, the National Academy of Sciences (NAS) undertook the job assigned to it by the same law. The Academy appointed a Committee on Motor Vehicle Emissions, composed of distinguished professionals not connected with the automobile industry — professors of engineering, medical men, industrial engineers.

This NAS Committee shares the doubts of automobile manufacturers about the catalytic converters. It reported that "the technology necessary to meet the requirements of the Clean-Air Amendments for 1975-model-year, light-duty motor vehicles is not available at this time." A majority of the committee concluded, however, that "the status of development and rate of progress make it possible that the larger manufacturers will be able to produce vehicles that will qualify." But, the Committee warned, the devices necessary for the required emission control will have a harmful and dangerous effect on engine performance: they will give engines a tendency to stall in traffic, and make them less capable of quick acceleration. Professor A. J. Haagen-Smit, chairman of the California Air Resources Board, says: "I hate to think of all the accidents that will occur when people try to drive these balky new cars up the ramps and into the fast flow of crowded freeways."

Once the devices are on cars, moreover, consumers cannot get rid of them. Under the clean-air law, a manufacturer can be fined $10,000 for not putting a pollution-abatement device on a car; and a consumer can be fined the same amount for taking one off.

Just when the balky new cars will go into production is at present uncertain. In 1972, manufacturers asked the EPA to grant a one-year extension of the requirement that all the new devices be installed under warranty for 1975-model cars. On April 11, 1973, EPA gave manufacturers a partial extension. The EPA ruled that catalytic converters need not be installed on all 1975-model cars, but must be installed on cars sold in California.

Ralph Nader (and some union bosses) denounced this partial extension of the deadline as a "sell-out to the big car industry" by the Nixon Administration, and threatened to go to court. Car manufacturers did go to court. They appealed the ruling as setting harsh, unattainable goals for them.

Testifying before a Senate Subcommittee, John Riccardo, president of Chrysler Corporation, said: "We very seriously believe catalytic converters are a mistake for this country and ought to be avoided." Riccardo pleaded with Congress to abandon the pollution-emission standards set under the clean-air law and to adopt standards set by the state of California, which has had the most experience with air pollution and pollution control. Riccardo said he thought the industry could meet the California standards by 1977, without the catalytic converters that must be added to meet federal standards.

The difference between the two sets of standards is very small in terms of pollutants in the air, but very large in terms of capital requirements and costs. Mobil Oil Corporation, supporting Riccardo's position, estimates that substituting California pollution-emission standards for federal standards would save American consumers $66 billion over a ten-year period — in lower cost of emission-control devices, lower costs for car maintenance, and better gasoline mileage. The substitution, according to Mobil's estimate, would also save the nation 30 million barrels of crude oil consumption in 1976, and 150 million barrels a year by 1980.

Congress has shown no sign of an intention to amend the clean-air act in the direction of sanity, although government enforcement officials themselves say the law should be changed. In announcing the partial extension of April 11, 1973, which car manufacturers appealed, the EPA director suggested that Congress "take another look" at the clean-air law before all its provisions are fully enforced on automobile manufacturers. Members of the NAS Committee on Motor Vehicle Emissions have made the same suggestion.

Unless public opinion induces Congress to "take another look" at the clean-air law, cumbersome new automobiles, laden with expensive (about $400 per car) but unproven emission-control devices, will eventually be rolling across the American landscape — conspicuous examples of economic and engineering decisions made for political reasons.

Devices on present cars have already increased fuel consumption by 4.6 percent — which means that present cars with emission-control devices are daily using 12.6 million gallons of gasoline more than they would be using without the devices. And the new models, when they come, will consume 20 percent more gasoline than today's new cars. Typically, having aggravated the energy crisis by requiring automobile manufacturers to build cars that consume more gasoline, the EPA in April 1973 criticized manufacturers for building cars that use too much gasoline, and proposed a new regulation requiring that new cars be labelled to show their expected fuel consumption.

Still, the biggest expense to consumers caused by the clean-air act could be for periodic inspections. Alexander Rihm Jr., director of New York's Air Pollution Control Program, says that inspecting a car to determine whether its emission-control devices meet federal standards will be a complex procedure. It will require sophisticated equipment costing about $15,000, and the services, not of garage mechanics, but of highly skilled technicians. "Can you imagine," Mr. Rihm asks, "what the expense would be and the inspection fees that would have to be charged if this type of testing were done at 11,000 inspection stations in New York State?"

The cost to taxpayers and consumers for an adequate network of inspection stations in all 50 states and the territories could run into billions of dollars. In the clean-air law, Congress did order the establishment of such a network, but failed to authorize funds. In fact, the law excuses motorists from using the inspection facilities which it requires to be provided. The clean-air law requires the EPA to establish testing procedures and to ensure that inspection and testing facilities are available to the public; but it provides that after a vehicle has been sold an inspection of its pollution-abatement devices may be made only with the owner's permission.

Apparently the Clean-Air Amendments Act was not intended to be an enforceable measure that would protect the public. It is most useful, however, as a weapon against an economic system that allows free enterprise to be regulated by the free choice of consumers.

Consumer advocates routinely assert that automobiles cause 60 percent of the problem of air pollution. Mr. Rihm says this assertion "is a *gross* [his emphasis] misrepresentation of the fact, and it results from people trying to make headlines by oversimplifying the total problem of air pollution." Mr. Rihm told of a Member of Congress (whom he declined to identify) publicly saying that cars cause 60 percent of air pollution. When challenged, the Congressman justified the "gross misrepresentation" by saying: "We have to use this figure so that laymen will understand us." Mr. Rihm indicates that cars may actually produce 4 to 10 percent of all harmful contaminants in the atmosphere.

Dr. Philip Handler, president of the National Academy of Sciences, says: "Overall, natural production of hydrocarbons, carbon monoxide, and perhaps NOX [nitrogen oxides] far exceeds that from man-made sources."

Car motors emit four basic substances that

the government is trying to outlaw as air-contaminants producing effects harmful to human beings and to all other life, plant and animal, and also to certain inorganic materials. The four substances are carbon monoxide, hydrocarbons, nitrogen oxides, and lead.

A 1972 report by the Environmental Protection Agency said that car emissions of carbon monoxide, hydrocarbons, and nitrogen oxides do great damage to "material and vegetation," but acknowledged that the cost of controls to eliminate these noxious emissions will be 8.1 times greater than the total cost of the damage the emissions cause. The EPA said it had made no estimate of health benefits to be derived from car-emission controls, "because of an almost complete lack of data" about the health effects of carbon monoxide, hydrocarbons, and nitrogen oxides in the general atmosphere.

How about the villain lead?

The first EPA regulation concerning lead required oil companies to make lead-free gasoline "generally available" to the public by mid-1974. An EPA regulation proposed in April 1973 would gradually reduce the allowable lead content of all gasoline until none contains lead. In November 1972, the EPA published a paper giving its reasons for regulating leaded gasoline out of existence. In a careful, scholarly analysis of this EPA paper, Dr. Harold H. Golz, medical director of the American Petroleum Institute, observes that the EPA makes assertions it does not even attempt to prove. The EPA's assertion that lead in the atmosphere has had harmful effects on health, Dr. Golz says, is "unwarranted, speculative, and unsupported by scientific evidence."

The federal bureaucracy is heaping enormous new costs on American consumers by requiring vast and sweeping changes in two major industries, oil and automotive manufacturing; is increasing both the cost and the consumption of energy fuels; and is accelerating the drive toward socialism by enlarging the sphere of illegal government controls in the marketplace — all with the single purpose of getting lead out of gasoline, though there is no reliable evidence that leaded gasoline does any harm.

Surely, if spending the public's money would give us clean air and solve our problems, by now we would have an antiseptic atmosphere and no problems. But political environmentalists have limitless capacity for bamboozling the public. A few years ago, one of them, Senator Gaylord Nelson (D.-Wisconsin), was predicting that unless we stopped pollution, city dwellers would be wearing breathing helmets by 1980, and the human race would be extinct by the year 2020. Since making such predictions, Nelson has supported federal environmental legislation which has piled many billions of dollars of continuing expense on the public. To justify what he has done, escape ridicule for his doomsday predictions, and get support for even more extravagant environmental spending, Senator Nelson is now saying that the costly programs he has supported in the past have saved humanity, have stopped its plunge into extinction, and have given it a little more time to create heaven on earth — if the public will submit to the additional raping of taxpayers that Senator Nelson recommends.

Chapter Thirteen

Is The Goose In The Oven?

HISTORICALLY, Socialism has an unbroken record of failure. Whenever it becomes total, it brings grinding poverty and crushing tyranny.

The American business system, on the other hand, has produced more prosperity, more widely distributed, than any other economic system has ever produced. It has created more schools, universities, art galleries, theaters, orchestras, publishing houses, churches, hospitals, clinics, beautiful parks, magnificent recreational facilities, comfortable dwellings, means of travel, and means of communication than have ever been enjoyed anywhere else.

But we could lose what we have. The American business system is under attack by forces that are dragging us into Socialism.

The Conference Board, an independent business-research organization, says business leaders are worried because "the image of private enterprise is being shaped by critics of the system."

In 1972, Opinion Research Corporation of Princeton, New Jersey, reported on a national opinion-sampling of the views of 4,059 persons, representing a cross-section of the total population. Opinion Research said that in seven years

(1965-1972), the proportion of the U.S. public expressing "low approval for business" rose from 47 percent to 60 percent. Other findings from Opinion Research polls include the following:

● The public at large believes that the after-tax profits of corporations average 28 percent. Even company stockholders think corporate profits average 23 percent after taxes. The average American thinks a 10 percent after-tax profit for corporations would be fair. (In reality, the actual average corporate after-tax profit is 4 percent).

● The public ranks corporate price increases as second only to the Vietnam War as the major cause of inflation.

● Even 60 percent of stockholders interviewed believe that competition cannot be counted on to keep prices at fair levels and that government controls are necessary.

● One-third of the U.S. public thinks the federal government should set ceilings on business profits.

● One-third of the U.S. public thinks that the most practical way for workers to improve their standard of living is to get more of the money companies are making, rather than to increase their own productivity.

● Fifty-three percent of the U.S. public feel that business is doing very little to combat pollution; 81 percent of consumers think plants that pollute the environment should be shut down; but only 22 percent said they would be willing to pay higher prices to cover the cost of installing pollution-control equipment. Most of those surveyed felt the cost should come out of business profits.

● Twenty percent of the public criticized corporations for not doing enough to maintain full employment; for not doing enough to hire and train Negroes; for not providing rewarding and satisfying jobs for workers; for not doing enough to help clean up the ghettoes; for not responding to the needs of the younger generation; for not providing day-care centers for preschool children whose mothers work.

Malcolm C. MacKinnon, executive vice president of United Gilsonite Laboratories, puts it bluntly: "People think business is no good."

And G.J. Tankersley, president of East Ohio Gas Company, sums up the situation in striking terms:

> Unless we keep prices at the most reasonable possible levels, the customer is going to walk away whether we are selling a hamburger or a supersonic aircraft. In too many cases, our nation's industries have simply been priced out of their markets.
>
> But how much have we done to convince Americans that keeping prices low is as vital to business as it is to any other segment of our society? They don't believe it . . . .
>
> Over a long period, management has steadily developed new techniques and methods to absorb vast increases in taxes, the cost of large wage and benefit packages, fantastic red tape, and proliferation of regulations, while at the same time, somehow, maintaining its ability

to build new facilities and provide more jobs.

There has been a feeling that, in America, it is simply impossible to kill or even slow down the industrial goose that lays the golden eggs of high employment. But, today, the goose may well be in the oven . . . .

Harassing business has become a major function of government; and much of the public has been induced to applaud and ask for more. For instance, government-caused spiraling of food prices was used to justify government controls to keep food prices down, but succeeded only in creating scarcity that made prices go even higher; government prohibitions against important business action brought on criticism of business for inaction, and still more government prohibitions. These illustrations reflect, not government bungling, but a deliberate stratagem in the war against free enterprise — a stratagem which has worked with classic precision during the Administration of Richard Nixon, who often gives fulsome praise to free enterprise.

Who is responsible? Oddly enough, leaders of the drive to destroy our business system are people on whom the system has showered the most benefits. Among them are intellectuals, who, thanks to business, have more freedom, leisure, and material means to be intellectuals than intellectuals have ever had anywhere else; also among the leaders are businessmen themselves.

Consider the Council on Foreign Relations (C.F.R.), which, together with many other tax-exempt organizations, has virtually run the United States Government since the 1940's. This cabal controls the major communications media, most of the opinion-influencing institutions, and many of the big businesses in the United States. It sets the major policies of the federal government; exercises controlling influence on government officials who implement the policies; and, through massive and skillful propaganda, influences Congress and the public to support the policies. Its objective is to establish a One World socialist system. Many members of the C.F.R., and of its interlocking affiliates, are businessmen.

Robert O. Anderson, for example, is chairman of the board of Atlantic Richfield — the oil company that drilled the discovery well on the Alaskan North Slope and was a leader in the bold, admirable Alaska pipeline venture. In 1969, Robert O. Anderson gave $80,000 to David R. Brower, a militant activist who organized Friends of the Earth. Friends of the Earth was one of the three political-environmental groups that stopped the Alaska pipeline with a lawsuit. The president of Atlantic Richfield is Thornton F. Bradshaw, a director of the Foreign Policy Association, one of the oldest, most important One World-socialist organizations interlocked with the C.F.R. Robert S. Ingersoll, a board member of Atlantic Richfield, is a trustee of the Aspen Institute for Humanistic Studies, another One World-socialist group. Ellmore C. Patterson, a board member of Atlan-

216

tic Richfield, is a trustee of the Carnegie Endowment for International Peace and a trustee of the Alfred P. Sloan Foundation, both sources of funds and leadership for militant New Left activists.

Standard Oil of New Jersey participated in the great Alaska oil-exploration and pipeline venture. Milo M. Brisco, president of Standard of New Jersey, was a member of the New York Urban Coalition when it was formed in 1967. The Urban Coalition is a militant socialist group. Donald S. MacNaughton, chairman and chief executive of Standard Oil of New Jersey, is on the policy council of Common Cause, a socialist consumer-advocate group.

Grayson L. Kirk, member of the board of Mobil Oil, another participant in the Alaska venture, is a director of the C.F.R. George C. McGhee, board member of Mobil, was a special assistant to the chairman of Urban Coalition in 1969-1970, and is now a director of the Aspen Institute for Humanistic Studies. Albert L. Williams, board member of Mobil Oil, is a trustee of the Alfred P. Sloan Foundation.

The owners and managers of the *New York Times*, a powerful publishing business, are leaders in the C.F.R. cabal; and they are financial backers of environmental groups that are harassing business in the United States. The *Times* has editorially condemned the Alaska pipeline venture as a new "South Sea Bubble" (a gigantic Eighteenth Century swindle in Great Britain). In the very same edition, the *Times* carried an article

217

eulogizing Siberian oil operations in the Soviet Union.

Members of many leading American business families (Rockefeller, Ford, Guggenheim, and others) are leaders in the movement that is detroying free enterprise.

Cyrus Eaton, wealthy Ohio industrialist, has been openly pro-Communist for many years. He calls himself "the Communists' favorite capitalist." Now, perhaps, David Rockefeller of the Chase Manhattan Bank and Armand Hammer of Occidental Petroleum both have a better claim to that title.

The accumulations of private wealth represented by these big businessmen are legal and desirable. If the meddling hand of government could be removed from economic activities, allowing all business to operate in a free market, controlled by consumers, the wealth of all businesses — large and small — would necessarily be used according to consumer demand. The meddling hand of government causes the problem.

Who is responsible for that meddling hand? Congress wrote, and in most cases the President approved, the laws that authorized all government activity. That fact exonerates big business, big unions, the C.F.R., the courts, and environmental groups from *basic* blame. They never elected a single Member of Congress. All their leaders combined do not have enough votes.

Are we to put all the blame on Congress and the President? No, we must go deeper than that.

No President or Member of Congress ever elected himself. The politicians whose laws are oppressing us were all elected by the people who do have enough votes to make decisions at the polls: little businessmen, big businessmen, workers, and their families. There is where the real blame must be laid: upon the voters who elected the politicians who wrote the laws.

The Sixteenth Amendment, which authorized our corrupt and oppressive federal income-tax system, was not adopted by wealthy unions, foundations, and other organizations exempt from taxation, or by the few wealthy individuals who escape taxation by crawling through legal loopholes. The income-tax amendment was adopted by low-and-moderate-income voters. They had been told that the progressive income-tax would ease their tax burden because it would soak the rich. Actually, the income-tax system soaks everyone except the favored few who are exempt. Low-and-moderate-income people pay most of the tax because there are more of them. The people were lied to about the income tax.

Nor is it the super-rich and the favored few who are basically responsible for the gigantic swindle called federal aid. The mass of voters support federal politicians who authorize the aid, and local politicians who make careers of getting it for their communities. The promise to voters is that "federal" money used locally eases their over-all tax load because it reduces their local and state taxes. But "federal" money is

219

also tax money, money confiscated from all Americans. When it is taken from local tax-payers and hauled to Washington, for redistribution as federal officials please, it shrinks in transit. What comes back as aid is a small fraction of what federal tax collectors take, and it comes with guidelines and controls attached. The people are being lied to about federal aid.

From this same mass of voters, whose majority decisions in elections are basically responsible for our problem, has also come, of course, the leadership and manpower for the resistance movement against total government; but more is needed. Businessmen are under special necessity to assume leadership in this movement.

A few big businessmen who join the big-union-big-government-big-business combine may survive — even thrive. But this is not free enterprise. It will end in economic degeneration, general poverty, and tyranny for everyone except an elite at the top. And some of the biggest businessmen will remain at the top, growing far more powerful. Expectation of such a position may, indeed, be the motivation behind their decisions. But the livelihood, as well as the freedom, of all other businessmen is doomed, if we do not halt our mad rush away from free enterprise.

Stating the job that must be done is easy: We must elect to Congress Constitutional conservatives who will trim the federal government down to Constitutional size, and limit it to the performance of Constitutional functions. Instead of trying to reform the antitrust programs and regulatory agencies, Congress should abolish them by repealing all the laws that created them. They are not needed. They do more harm than good. And they are all unconstitutional.

Doing the job that must be done is not easy. Many are discouraged from trying because they do not know where to start. A good place to start is at the bottom.

Harmful federal programs are so big and numerous, and the forces behind them so powerful, that resistance often seems futile. Trimming down the federal government by hacking at individual programs is somewhat like getting into the top of a big tree and trying to save it from a choking, fast-growing vine by cutting off the vine's uppermost tentacles. True, that is important. Whatever else may be done for the tree, eventually the vine wrapped around the upper branches must be removed. But if we want to stop the growth of the noxious vine so that we can cut it away faster than it grows, we must kill it. The only way to kill it is to cut it off at the roots.

Proliferating government programs are the vine that is choking the life out of the tree of our Constitutional government. This vine is rooted in a conspiracy of collectivists out to destroy the American free enterprise system. It is nourished largely by the federal income tax system. By ignoring the basics of our Constitution and by utilizing the resources furnished by the tax system, the conspirators have cultivated the vine until today its tentacles threaten to choke business out of existence and destroy Constitutional government. Some businessmen are aware of this but many more must become so. They must come to realize that if the income tax system were abolished, the conspiracy would be critically weakened, the size of government would greatly diminish, and most of the problems besetting business today could be resolved.

With income tax eliminated, the tax exemptions and special privileges that government now gives to powerful and wealthy interests would end. Politicians could no longer get elected by promising some voters gifts of tax money confiscated from other voters. Thousands of federal employees now consuming taxes as regulators of businesses and workers, and as dispensers of their tax money, would become part of the business community, which produces goods and services that consumers want. Millions of welfare "clients" who have never paid direct taxes and never will under the present system, who are being supported by taxes, and who are being organized (with government help) into militant lobbies demanding more tax money — these millions would have to go to work. With government off its back, business could create jobs for them, and most welfare recipients could thus become productive members of society. Then, an affluent society, without governmental interference, would take care of those unable to care for themselves.

The enemies of freedom engage in bitter

222

power struggles among themselves. The closer they come to total victory, the more continuous and mutually destructive their internecine fights become. Nonetheless, they always join forces in the main battle. In their jurisdictional struggles among themselves, the monopolistic unions murder and maim one another like gangsters; but they stand together in a solid front to lobby for federal legislation like OSHA. Democrat and Republican politicians in Congress, too, shriek abuse at each other, and behave somewhat like gangsters; but they join hands to deliver overwhelming votes for programs destructive of free enterprise.

The friends of free enterprise often lack this cohesiveness on main issues. They tend to fight alone, each trying to save freedom in his particular corner. But freedom cannot be won or maintained that way, because freedom is not divisible.

The enemies of freedom have another characteristic deserving of emulation: patient persistence. When, early in this century, they began to move in important ways to destroy private capitalism in America, socialists were few in number, a ragtag bunch without financial resources, generally held in contempt — while businessmen enjoyed prestige. To accomplish their purpose, the conspirators had to use capitalism's wealth against capitalism, and enlist wealthy businessmen as leaders in the effort. Patient and relentless, they succeeded. Norman Thomas, long-time head of the Socialist Party, and Earl Browder, long-time head of the Communist Party, both said, before they died, that there was no longer any need for them and their organizations to participate directly in American political campaigns, because Democrats and Republicans had adopted all their basic programs.

The goose that laid the golden eggs is in trouble. She may not be in the oven yet; but the poor creature, already severely plucked by government, is cornered, menaced by many foes with sharp and gleaming axes. Rescuing her will take courage, as well as effort.

There are businessmen who are afraid to distribute books like this one, and other documents that tell the freedom story and the story of the conspiracy to destroy it. They are afraid to cancel their advertising in publications and on TV and radio broadcast programs that reveal an anti-business bias; afraid to buy advertising space in magazines that are known for their stalwart stand against big government; afraid to support patriotic educational organizations to bring the message of what is happening to the people. They fear such actions will lose them customers, stir up the unions against them, invite the unfriendly attention of government agencies. They have reason to fear. But if they will not put aside their fear and act honorably in their own larger interests, their goose will surely be cooked. It is for this very reason that they must join forces with each other and with their employees — must unite with the many thousands of Americans already working to save free enterprise while there still is time.

Index

This index is a brief general guide to key information in the book, and is not, therefore, a complete list of all names and topics mentioned.

231